"We've slept through a rev[...] heeded, we will lose an enti[...] *The Pro-Teen Parent,* has n[...] underscores workable solutions. It's a book about helping teens develop and implement a rationale for responsible behavior.

"Hands-on, gutsy, succinct, and practical are terms that describe the contents of this book. Filled with amply illustrated principles, it teaches and illustrates ways to bring teens to embrace biblical values.

"I highly recommend it. I believe thousands of parents will find practical, tested, workable solutions to the problems of guiding teens towards biblical maturity."

—JOSEPH C. ALDRICH, *President*
Multnomah School of the Bible

"Powerful reading. This book is for everyone who loves teenagers . . . not just parents, but youth pastors and youth workers as well."

—MIKE TROUT
Christian Broadcaster

"*The Pro-Teen Parent* is a must-have resource for every parent of an adolescent! Parents learn how to help their teens develop a faith of their own, how to impart a sense of right and wrong, and how to motivate them to make wise choices.

"Dr. Hahn has written a tremendously practical book that we enthusiastically recommend. Your teen can love and obey God even during those tumultuous teenage years!"

—ARAM AND MARGIE KEITH
The Keith Companies

"*The Pro-Teen Parent* is one of the best 'coaching manuals' for Christian parents that I have ever read. It is not just another book on youth culture or discipline of teens. It is a broad and balanced handbook that addresses all dimensions of spiritual development.

"I recommend the book because it is thoroughly biblical, very readable, practical, relevant, and insightful. It affirms our parental role as the most significant influence on our teens.

As a parent of three (soon to be four) adolescents, I can tell you that the principles in this book work. As a youth pastor for ten years, I can vouch for the accuracy of Dr. Hahn's insights into the culture, minds, and lives of teens at the end of the twentieth century. As a family ministries pastor, this work is one that I recommend to every Christian parent of teens. As an elder, I feel every church leader should evaluate their ministries in light of the observations herein.

"*The Pro-Teen Parent* is a wonderful reflection of Dr. Hahn's ministry that he is unselfishly sharing with us all."

—DOUG HAAG, *Associate Pastor, Family Ministries*
First Evangelical Free Church, Fullerton, California

THE PRO-TEEN PARENT

The 10 Best Ways to Cheer On Your Teen's Growth in God

DANIEL M. HAHN

QUESTAR PUBLISHERS, INC.

The Pro-Teen Parent
© 1992 by Questar Publishers, Inc.

Printed in the United States of America
International Standard Book Number: 0-945564-57-0

Cover Illustration by Steve Björkman

Most Scripture quotations are from the New International Version
(©1973, 1978, 1984 by International Bible Society;
used by permission of Zondervan Publishing House).

This book is dedicated to
Lori and Katie, who have filled the longings
of my heart with love; and to Dave,
my friend, who has filled
the canyons of my life with laughter.

ACKNOWLEDGMENTS

The positive principles contained in these pages were modeled by my own family as I grew up. To them I am eternally grateful. Since then, godly men like David Needham at Multnomah School of the Bible, Chuck Swindoll and Doug Haag at the First Evangelical Free Church of Fullerton, and Jack Monroe and Jay Marshall of Mission Hills Church have poured boundless time and energy into my life, thinking, and ministry.

Without the editorial expertise of Gretchen Passentino, Boyd Luter, and Bill Watkins, the initial manuscript would have been indecipherable. Without the vision, commitment, and skill that Stephen Barclift, Don Jacobson, Dan Rich, David Uttley, and Thomas Womack of Questar poured over this project, it would have never come to fulfillment. Without the belief and encouragement of my in-laws, Bob and Bette Ring, I would have shelved my dreams numerous times. Without the tireless, extra-mile attitude of my secretary, Mary Lou Hardenbrook, and my assistant, Mark Strecker, I would never have found the time to put these thoughts down on paper. And finally, without the insight and support of the teens and families of Mission Hills Church, I would have nothing to say. They have been my wisest teachers.

CONTENTS

PREFACE

For over a decade now, I have listened to the honest concerns of loving parents, as well as the spiritual cries of disillusioned teens. In addition, I dedicated my post-graduate studies toward gaining a better understanding of just these special people. But the book you hold is written from a vantage point I'll never have again: I'm still quite young. I haven't forgotten that much. The wounds I endured during my teen years still throb from time to time. The elations I experienced still ring in my ears.

Beyond what I remember so clearly, I have the advantage of being able to spend countless hours each week with a large number of teenagers from widely varying family backgrounds. This broad spectrum of contact affords a great deal of perspective. I play video games with these kids, surf with them, go camping with them, eat lunch with them, and pray with them. We can connect. To some degree, I know that the passing of years will march me farther from their world. I'll gain some ground and lose some by becoming a parent of a teenager myself. I'll mature one perspective by living it, and diminish another one by leaving it behind.

For now, much of my time not spent with teenagers is spent with their parents. They share their tales and we laugh—so that we don't cry. We talk a lot of shop. We look at problems and discuss solutions. We enjoy each other's company in what can, at times, seem like war. I really love these parents of the teens I serve. They are the ones who have encouraged me to write. They have insightfully pointed out that this may be the only time in my life that I'll be able to see both sides so clearly.

The pages that follow are intended for Christian adults who are, or soon will be, in contact with teenagers on a regular basis — parents of teens (or soon-to-be teens), grandparents, Sunday School teachers, small group leaders, youth pastors, as well as leaders in Christian youth organizations. People who are deeply interested in helping teens move closer to embracing a tangible faith.

This book is about helping teenagers develop a rationale for responsible behavior in a culture that often encourages the opposite. It's about ways to help them embrace godly values—like honesty, integrity, and purity—and make moral choices, even when it isn't convenient. It's about the challenges we adults encounter during the process of instilling those values—challenges like disciplining, communicating, and freeing them to try their wings. We'll deal with those heart issues that constitute a teenager's budding spiritual life as it confronts and clashes with the real world.

That's why I've written about teenagers from a real-world perspective—because understanding them is so key to helping them. We'll be prying open the lid on the lives of five very real teens who come from homes like those of people you know. We'll journey through adolescence with these five teens, along the way adding the perspectives of others. We'll see their parents as these teens see them. And we'll look at their feelings, fears, and spiritual wars.

It's my prayer that God will use this book in a powerful way to encourage, guide, and stimulate your own thinking, in order to meet the challenges you face with the teenagers you love. And if that happens, I'll be "stoked."

INTRODUCTION

I was sitting at my dining room table with a cup of coffee, my face buried in a book, when I was jerked upright by a blast outside. It sounded like a car had blown up. I retied the terry cloth belt on my bathrobe and walked to the door to look outside. As though some eerie space invader had lured me away from my house, I stepped outside, eyes glued northward, up the street. What I saw was awesome, immense, beautiful, and frightening all at once. Mt. St. Helens had erupted. Hiroshima revisited!

As I stood there shivering in the street, along with my half-dressed neighbors, a black canopy of ash began to spread out over the sky like a curtain drawn across the state of Washington. A few of my neighbors ran back inside to turn on their radios for information.

I barely made it to church that morning, and I may as well have stayed home anyway. The lesson I had prepared for the college class blurred into the background. After all, who cares about a little man named Zacchaeus when the sky is falling?

In the days that followed, Portland was covered with powdery volcanic ash. No one knew what to do with it. The flakes just kept falling like grey, dry snow, eventually blanketing everything. The fine dust clogged carburetors, billowed up behind moving vehicles, and introduced a cleanup nightmare never before experienced in the Northwest.

Hitting adolescence is similar. For years, everything has gone fine. Childhood seems to be reasonably predictable and manageable. Then, without much warning, puberty erupts with the force of a volcanic blast. Changes take place across the landscape of a kid's life like never before. Everyone around is stunned and left reeling, not sure how to respond appropriately.

But adolescence is more than just an explosion. It's an awesome and wonderful break from the constraints of childhood into a whole new world of physical, mental, emotional, social, and spiritual capabilities. At age thirteen, I discovered that love was more than just a deep admiration for my math teacher. I suddenly realized that I had a range of feelings I'd never experimented with before. I noticed for the first time that I was part of a bigger world than I had ever imagined.

I also began to question all that stuff I'd heard in Sunday school. Suddenly the little boxes that contained my perceptions of God and the world about me were expanding. I was arguing and thinking and worrying about what was and wasn't going to characterize my life. Literally everything about myself and the way I interpreted the world changed with dizzying speed and force. I felt like Dorothy when the tornado hit home.

Teenage turmoil blankets those closest by with words, attitudes, reactions, and accusations that startle, frighten, and irritate adults, who are more predictable. In the wake of the blast we ask, "What do we do now?" Volumes have been written about the physical and social dimensions of adolescence, while often the spiritual maze of a teenager's life goes undiscussed. I can understand that. In the past, teens have often been stereotyped as having little spiritual interest. Youth groups have traditionally been thought of as a wild and crazy holding tank to occupy teenagers while their parents go to church (or sleep in). Only recently has the diagnosis changed.

Parents, caring adults who work with teens, educators, and church leaders are waking up to the fact that adolescence is the primary spawning ground for a person's spiritual life. The spiritual and moral formation that occurs during the teenage years molds attitudes and actions that are rarely tampered with, once adulthood has been cemented in place. For people who care about the destiny of teenagers, nothing is more important than nurturing the development of faith and values in a fresh generation.

But the road is a rough one. As I sit here on my porch writing, I can see beyond the patio table a blooming hibiscus I planted just weeks ago. The plant was raised to be healthy, and has appeared to flourish during its residence on my veranda. Yet upon closer inspection, it is very clear that its beautiful blossoms are under siege! That's right. Hundreds, perhaps thousands, of tiny aphids have infiltrated. The plant is covered with them. Like Hitler's men they're marching along, eating and destroying the plant as they go. Unless I intervene, the plant will be eaten alive. It will die in its prime.

More serious is the spiritual and moral infestation sweeping across America. Like a brush fire, it is fueled by the wind of monetary gain and sustained by the natural passions we all experience. Just as life is blossoming, sin seems to wrap its ugly fingers around the necks of our adolescents. Many are seriously wounded. Some don't survive.

Teenagers are discovering this earlier than we ever did. While they're attempting to wrap the world around themselves, they're sensing an inner emptiness that is vast and frightening. If they don't find a stable center, another axis, life will cave in.

Many teenagers are, in fact, caving in. They're opting out in record numbers. Suicides among fifteen- to nineteen-year-olds have risen over 400 percent in the last decade, with over 600,000 teens attempting suicide in one year. Every minute in America another teenager attempts to take his own life, and every hour someone under the age of twenty-five will succeed.[1]

Does it look bleak? Does it bother us just a little? Does it bother us enough to grope for some answers? Is it possible to ford this moral wasteland and instill values of love, goodness, and responsibility in a fresh generation of young people? How do we go about communicating a solid foundation of faith and values in this cosmopolitan culture, in this crazy period of history? That's what this book is all about. There are real, workable answers, if we're willing to fight the current to find them.

In order to put these answers in a tangible context, let me take you somewhere you may have never traveled. I'd like you to imagine that the book you're holding is somewhat like C.S. Lewis's wardrobe that leads to another world. Let's journey from life as we adults know it into the fascinating world of another generation. But I must warn you: The world on the other side of this wardrobe is real. The characters are real. The places are real. The events are real. Only the names and incidental details have been altered in order to protect individuals' privacy. Now step inside and meet five of my friends who live on the other side.

GARY CAME TO OUR student gathering off and on. More off than on, actually. I'd joke with him, we'd talk about school and his struggles with the principal, and he'd laugh when I'd ask him if he had a girlfriend. But then Gary wouldn't show again for a month or two. It was one warm summer evening, just after our midweek youth meeting had started, that I met the "other" Gary for the first time.

He and some friends had cracked open a six-pack in the back of a pickup truck in the church parking lot. Word got around the group that they were out there drinking, so I went out to talk with them. As I approached the truck, they slid their beers underneath a blanket (as if I was blind) and mumbled something like, "Don't say anything" (as if I was deaf). I tried some sort of greeting, and just got half-blank, half-angry stares in return. Gary snapped that they weren't doing anything wrong and were just leaving. Despite my attempt to engage them in a conversation, they insisted they had to leave. My phone messages after that night were never returned.

Four months later I saw Gary again. He'd come to our Wednesday night meeting, this time to look for someone. He had his "bro's" with him. They searched through the swarm of 200 or so students and picked out one. It was right about then that word reached me. "Gary and some of the guys from the gang he's in are here. They're taking Larry Jenson around to the back of the church to beat him up."

I caught the mob on their way toward the dark part of the church parking lot. "Wait, Gary . . . " Before I could say anything else, he stopped, turned around, and with a glare that could melt steel, shoved Larry toward me, accompanied by a four-letter expletive. "This is none of your business," he blasted. "We're just payin' him back, that's all." Again, before I could say a word, he angrily mumbled, "We'll leave, don't worry, we'll leave." His stare focused on Larry, with just brief glances toward me. But that October night, standing there next to a shivering Larry, I saw something more than anger in Gary's eyes. While I couldn't have proven it then, I was sure I had seen something else, someone else—a kid who had lost all sense of power in his life and was desperately trying to win it back.

EVER SINCE I'VE KNOWN Karen she's been something of a recluse. A few years ago, Karen began opening up a little. But everything that came out was negative. She hated school. Her folks were too restrictive. No one liked her. She was ugly. Or so she said in many different ways, over and over. She was constantly sick. The saddest part, I discovered, was that she was engaged in a downward spiral that confirmed her self-depreciation.

Karen's depression was affecting her school attendance and homework; so getting parent notices and bad report cards, of course, gave her a reason to dislike school. Her parents were trying desperately to help her improve by restricting her social life so that she would get better grades. Naturally, then, she simply saw them as overbearing and the culprits behind her impoverished relationships. To console herself, Karen increasingly became engrossed in television, and inhaled junk food like it was air. She didn't get any exercise. So she gained weight. Her health problems worsened. At one point she called my wife and I to inform us that she was ready to commit suicide. In effect, she had become what she accused herself of being—a mess and a loser.

LET ME INTRODUCE YOU to another friend. Sarah was a senior at a continuation school when I met her. At the age of 19 she was getting her GED, after having dropped out of school at 15. Sarah worked as a waitress. Her hair was slightly orange and her combat boots looked funny under her plaid skirt, but the lost look on her face was beginning to fade. It was being replaced with a resilient and genuine smile.

Sarah's parents divorced when she was seven and her baby brother was two. Her dad left the state soon after, and since the day he walked out the door she has only seen him twice. Her mom has had numerous boyfriends, some of whom have lived in their cramped apartment from time to time. Sarah has forgotten much of her life back then. She vaguely remembers helping her drunken mom up the stairs and into their apartment. And she has random recollections of how one of her mother's boyfriends, who was living with them at the time, used to slide his hand up under her dress and whisper, "Big girls don't mind."

But for the most part, the years past have all been tucked away in boxes that, for the present, are too painful to look into. Just recently, a few of the boxes have opened ever so slightly. Through the loving assistance of a skilled counselor, Sarah is working through the excruciating process of healing and forgiveness. For the first time in years, Sarah is drug and alcohol free. She's chipping away at a massive wall of bitterness that had imprisoned her. And she's discovering that God hasn't given up on her. That's what keeps her going.

RANDY'S FAMILY HAS ATTENDED our church since before he was born. Randy's mom, Jean, has been the instigator of what has become an annual crafts fair on the front lawn of the church. She also works tirelessly in the nursery, and has taught various Sunday school classes from time to time. In fact, Randy recalls being in a few of her classes over the years. He told me about the time he and some friends used black felt-tip markers to add beards and mustaches to the women in his mom's flannel-graph story right before class. She was obligated to use them, beards and all, and the fourth-grade boys Sunday school class was never the same.

I consider Dennis, Randy's dad, a good friend. He's served on the elder board of our church two different terms, and has been a strong supporter of our youth programs. Since Randy was young, he's gone fishing and hunting with his dad. In fact, Dennis bought a ski boat, and the family has taken full advantage of their time together over the years.

By the time Randy got to high school, he and I had grown pretty close. We'd tackled rock climbing and white-water rafting, and challenged each other to plenty of wrestling matches (which I won by sheer weight) on the youth room floor. Randy was what I'd call a really good kid from a really secure family. That was Randy's ninth-grade year—the year before his life became a roller coaster. I'll tell you why in just a bit.

FINALLY, MEET JIMMY, WHO began attending our church as a junior high student. From his very first day in our group, he seemed agitated. He twirled his pencil. He poked holes in his lesson outlines. He made trip after trip to the rest room, or the drinking fountain, or just out to the hall to see what else was going on. During our class discussions he would stare upward counting ceiling tiles, while the other students were tracking with me. He had the attention span of a hummingbird.

I tried to communicate with Jimmy's parents, but both worked full-time and were busy most evenings, so setting up an appointment with them was futile. We finally arranged a conference call after two weeks of playing phone tag. "I know what you mean," Jimmy's dad concurred. "He has the same problem at school, and we're always getting calls." Elaine, Jimmy's mom, explained, "We've had him tested and retested for physical and emotional problems but nothing really shows up. They say he's just hyperactive, but not bad enough to warrant medication. He's just a little wild. It drives me crazy at home."

On a Sunday morning shortly after our phone conversation, Jimmy showed up for the junior high gathering a little early. He was hanging out by the coke machine in the entry hall when I walked by with a stack of papers in my hand. Reaching out to give him a "high five" greeting, I dropped the papers and they scattered on the floor. We laughed and got on our hands and knees to retrieve my stack. Somewhere down there on the floor we found ourselves engrossed in a conversation. We wound up leaning against the cinder block wall, talking about his favorite band, soccer, school, and what he was thinking and feeling.

"I get in trouble a lot and my parents get mad at me," Jimmy explained cautiously.

"What do you get in trouble for?" I asked.

"Nothing. The teachers just pick on me. I talk too much, I guess."

"What do your parents say about that?"

"Nothing. They just get mad."

"Do you ever try to tell them how you're feeling?"

"Not really."

"Why is that?"

"They never listen to me."

Soon we were getting up off the floor to head into the meeting room, when Jimmy added, "My dad is gone most of the time . . . so that's good." Without saying anything else, he walked off to look for his friends.

NOW THAT YOU'VE MET my friends, we're ready to walk into their world. As we do, I believe you'll agree we're about to encounter a new level of perspective and purpose for the task at hand.

NOTE:

1. Paul W. Swets, How to Talk So Your Teenager Will Listen (Dallas: Word, 1988), p. 122.

SOMETHING ON THE INSIDE

Be Alert to Your Teenager's Spiritual Searching

Ever feel like your teenager's spiritual life is nonexistent? Look *again. It may be that the reality of faith is closer than you* *think. Even when you can't see it, a kid's spiritual journey is* *very real. He needs your help now, more than ever.*

I jerked awake and tried to focus my eyes on the lighted clock display: 1:10 A.M. The phone rang again. A frantic mother on the other end began describing her son's behavior. "Daniel, you've got to help me. Gary is going wild. We can't control him. He was at a party with one of his friends. They came home and he's completely out of control. He's kicking things and yelling, more like screaming." Her voice trailed and lowered to a whisper. "He just walked back in the front door," she continued. "He knows I'm talking to you . . . he says *he* wants to talk to you." I waited, still trying to orient myself to the situation.

I heard someone pick up the receiver on the other end. "Hi, Gary?" I asked. The reply was something I was hardly pre-pared for. There were no real words, just a heavy growling and raspy breathing. It sounded as though he was trying to form words but couldn't quite get them out. It was frightening.

My wife overheard the sounds coming from the phone and sat up in bed next to me. "What's going on?" she whispered.

His mother came back on the phone. "I think you'd better get down here."

It was nearly 1:45 A.M. when I neared Gary's home. Ahead of me, red and blue lights bounced off surrounding houses. I pulled up behind the sheriff's car and got out. In the dimness of the street light, I could see Gary's form flattened out on the driveway. His wrists were handcuffed behind his back, his shirt was torn to shreds. His dad and mom were kneeling on either side of Gary, holding on to his shoulders. A phalanx of cops and paramedics surrounded the three of them.

Gary's chest was heaving up and down as I bent close to him. He immediately recognized me, though his eyes were glassy and distant.

"Don't touch me," countered a strange hissing voice I'd never heard before. He struggled away from his father and sat up.

I held his legs with my arm to avoid being kicked and looked directly into his eyes. "Gary, Gary!" He looked away into the sky. I took hold of his face and directed his gaze toward me.

He jerked back. "You don't have any power over me," he growled. "Let me go, I've got to kill them!"

"Who, Gary? Who do you have to kill?"

"All of them," he shot back. "All those cops, I've got to kill them. I've got to kill you, too."

I knew Gary well. The voice was not his. I began talking directly to whatever power had overtaken him. "Who are you?" I demanded. "What is your name?" The only response I got was, "I can't tell you."

Holding him down with one arm and the weight of my body, I nervously flipped through my Bible to Mark 5, and began reading about how Christ had delivered the demon-possessed man from his madness. Immediately Gary arched his back and screeched in some other voice, "Stop reading that, stop reading that! You have no power over me!" I continued to read through the passage and pled with Gary to be open to God's intervention on his behalf. Pressing his head next to mine, I prayed. I prayed for God to show Himself powerful. I prayed for all evil forces to depart. I prayed for a miracle. The pleading, the praying, the fitful outbursts just dragged on for what seemed like hours.

From time to time, Gary would relax slightly. At one point he looked at me like a frightened child just waking from a nightmare. But within moments he was swept away again by some wave of insanity, and would begin writhing, growling, and spewing out threats all over again.

Paramedics belted Gary onto a stretcher and headed to Valley Hospital, where tests were conducted in the emergency room. I waited with his folks until word reached us. Gary had consumed some alcohol, but not a trace of drugs was detected. The doctors had no explanation. They assured us the alcohol could not have elicited the type of reaction they had witnessed. It was something else. They just didn't know what.

In the days that followed, Gary had milder reoccurrences, separated by periods when he seemed just fine. I continued to pray for him. I fasted. I asked others to pray. Finally I ended up spending the night at Gary's home and talked with him well into the morning. I shared experiences from my own life, and prayed with him for deliverance. That night I discovered something that changed my perspective. Gary told me what it was like to feel the power and the intrigue of all that was happening inside of him. He was actually, in a strange sort of way, enjoying it. I realized then that no permanent change would occur until Gary was willing to submit his heart to the love of God. No one could do it for him.

AN UNSEEN REALITY

Over the centuries, demonic activity has been blatant in some cultures, more secretive in others. In just the past few years, satanism and occult practices have come to the forefront of American teen culture in an unprecedented way. Movies which are marketed to appeal to adolescents are replete with seances, witches, spirits of the dead, impersonal cosmic forces, life after death, and demons that stalk their victims. Most teenagers I know can quote songs laced with lyrics which blatantly honor

Satan and all that he stands for. The occult is experiencing an upsurge in our own nation like never before, and its primary target is teenagers.

This is not the world you grew up in. It's not the same safe, materialistic, predictable world of even twenty years ago. The "supernatural," so we thought, just happened in other, much more uncivilized, countries. You know: spiritualists, demonic outbreaks, belief in reincarnation, meditation, inner healing through mind control, and all that strange stuff. All of that's over in India, or at least down in Haiti, right? Welcome to the new unseen reality. The spirit world is alive and well, and American teens are plugging into it.

Not long ago, I was browsing through a popular bookstore. Positioned prominently was an enormous section on religion. The top shelf included numerous copies of Anton LeVey's *Satanic Bible*. The section trailed into books on world religions, followed by a fifteen-foot-long stretch dedicated to mysticism, the occult, and New Age philosophies.

As I ran my hand along the titles, verses I had read for years came to mind in a whole new way:

"Satan himself masquerades as an angel of light" (2 Corinthians 11:14).

"The god of this age has blinded the minds of unbelievers, so that they cannot see the light of the gospel of the glory of Christ, who is the image of God" (2 Corinthians 4:4).

"Your enemy the devil prowls around like a roaring lion looking for someone to devour" (1 Peter 5:8).

So is this all there is? Just the dark side? Hardly. I have never been more amazed than I am right now at the way teenagers everywhere are turning from the darkness and heading directly into the light. In my own church of about 700 adults, for example, more than 250 teens show up every week to study Scripture, worship with intensity, pray for each other, and prepare to live lives that honor God! Why? Because they know that the spiritual dimension of life is *real.* They know they're in a battle. They know that their eternal lives, and the lives of their friends, are at stake.

SUPERNATURAL TURNAROUND

The Bible introduces us to a unique young kid named Josiah. As a teenager, something powerful took root in his heart, and it changed everything about the nation he was to rule.

The past had been pockmarked with horror. Josiah's grandfather, Manasseh, had built pagan altars. He had led the Israelite people into a flagrant mockery of the living God: He encouraged idol worship, practiced sorcery, and led seances.

As one would expect, Manasseh's son Ammon followed suit. "He did evil in the eyes of the Lord, as his father Manasseh had done . . . he worshiped the idols his father had worshiped . . . He forsook the Lord." But his revelry was a short fling. His own officials plotted his murder, and his reign came to a grisly end. He left behind only one good thing—a son named Josiah.

The national demise would have continued except for the fact that Josiah experienced a change of heart. Simply put, "he turned to the Lord — with all his heart and with all his soul and with all his strength." With a massive sweep, Josiah scoured the land with righteousness. Idols were demolished. Temples were leveled. Satanism came to a halt. And in time, life began to stir again among a people whose faith was being restored (see 2 Kings 21—23).

Anyone looking on the day that Ammon died would have predicted, "same song, third verse." After all, from birth Josiah had been steeped in the cesspool of debauchery accumulated by previous generations. The conditioning was all in place. The example had been crystallized forever. Or had it? Under normal conditions, nothing would have changed. In all the universe, only one potion could have broken the spell of evil that appeared to be insoluble. And what was that? A scrawny teenager, a powerful God, and a change of heart—three ingredients that dispelled the dark.

You met Sarah. She is beginning to pull a "Josiah move" in her own life. She is breaking through "this present darkness" to embrace a world of light.

She was "doing" guys, dealing drugs, dodging the authorities, and defending everything about her way of life. No one would have believed change was on the horizon. Not her friends. Not her guidance counselor. Not even me. But deep down inside somewhere there was a tiny speck of receptivity. And then one day the improbable became the incredible. Hell broke loose of Sarah's heart and she became a new creation in Christ. It was as if God himself was taking delight in showing us all that what is impossible within man is to be expected with God.

Do you still believe in the possible? In the supernatural? In a powerful God that keeps shining streams of light into a dark world?

A change of heart doesn't come easily or cheaply for most teenagers. It usually takes sweaty prayers during some awfully long nights on the part of some very dedicated parents. It usually involves a few committed others who light the path—and help clean up the messes. For most, the path toward faith isn't covered with rose petals. Rather, it's stained with tears.

FAITH—WHERE THE JOURNEY UPWARD BEGINS

For kids like Randy, faith in God is a concept they've been taught since before they can remember. For others, like Sarah, it's a drastic turning point in life, like a light turning on in a void of spiritual mayhem. But however it dawns, it's the explanation for so much of our confusion. It gives us the capacity to embrace God's Truth about life and relationships. It ushers in a new spiritual dimension of living, whereby love can take root. In God's eyes, every single human life is a potential relationship with Himself. He values each of us individually and equally. R.C. Sproul wrote about this:

> **Man's dignity rests in God who assigns an inestimable worth to every person. Man's origin is not an acci-**

dent, but a profoundly intelligent act by One who has eternal value; by One who stamps His own image on each person. God creates men and moves heaven and earth to redeem them when they fall. Our origin is in creation and our destiny is for redemption. Between these points every human heartbeat has value.[1]

That is exactly what teenagers are searching for: love, a feeling of being needed, purpose, and hope. Are we helping them make the connection between their natural needs and God's ability to meet them? When I talk to teens, it is usually about these very basic-to-life issues. It sinks in . . . slowly. In time, however, most teens grasp how God meets their needs and fulfills their longings—the basics of faith.

Teenagers need to hear the truth from us. They need to know we were designed by God. We were fashioned for relationship, not dropped alone and by happenstance into a huge universe. We were given dignity and freedom of choice by a Creator who intended something more from us than mechanical responses. God's goal was to have a relationship with a creature who would freely love Him.

But a deception was introduced by God's opponent, Satan, in the Garden of Eden. It was short and appeared to be sweet: "Disobey God. Do your own thing. Seek independence from your Creator. Break that relationship — and you'll be just fine. In fact, you'll be better off. You can be your own God." God had warned Adam and Eve. Independence from Him and His moral code for survival would bring about death. God was right.

"Sin entered the world through one man, and death through sin, and in this way death came to all men, because all sinned" (Romans 5:12).

The rest is history. We bought the line then and people buy it today. The "new age" movement is the same "old age" movement that's always been around, but in another costume: "Truth is found within yourself. Joy is found in self-actualization. Peace comes by focusing inward. You can be your own

God"—or so some say . . . just as some have always said. And the result of our independence is to "crash and burn." Literally. Religious rituals don't help. Self-actualization doesn't cut it. Personal discipline leaves us empty inside. There is nothing we can do about it on our own.

KAREN TOOK ME OUT to show me her new Honda. This was the first spark of something positive I'd seen in a long time. As she opened the car door, the smell of "new" wafted upward. "Get in," she demanded. "It's not what I wanted but I only have to pay for the insurance—my dad's making the payments, so *that's* cool."

I sat admiringly behind the wheel and asked if it came with an air bag. Karen got in on the passenger side. I reached up and grabbed a crystal prism that hung from her rear-view mirror. "What's this?" I inquired.

"Oh, everybody's got those. I don't know. It doesn't, like, *mean* anything or anything. You know, it just looks cool. It makes colors and stuff when the light shines through it."

I asked again, "Is it a 'new age' thing or what?"

Karen gazed at it. "One of my friends is into that stuff but I don't really believe it. She gave me that. She, like, goes to a store that sells books on magic and stuff. I don't know. I suppose some of it could be true. She's got a lot of personal problems, though. Like, I do too, I guess."

Karen is swimming in a sea of ideas—ideas that sound new, and full of possibilities and meaning. I spoke with her as we rode through a maze of tract houses. She revealed more of the aimlessness she felt at this point in her life. As we pulled back into the church parking lot, I said, "You know, Karen, I believe that the closer you get to the One who wired you, the more life is going to make sense. Do you believe that?"

"I'm not sure," Karen said softly. "But I'll think about it."

Satan is the purveyor of counterfeits. Magical solutions. Quick, self-actualizing fixes. But through the fog of fads, God's offer of eternal life remains. He's ready and willing to fill the void in young hearts with Himself. That's what makes the "Good News" so good—it's the plan of salvation and redemption. The only One who could secure that kind of a transformation for man was God's Son: "For God so loved the world that he gave his one and only Son, that whoever believes in him shall not perish but have eternal life" (John 3:16).

Faith is the link that bonds us once again with our Creator—faith in God's provision of Jesus Christ as our Savior. "Through faith, we have peace with God through our Lord Jesus Christ" (Romans 5:1).

This understanding of faith is critical to creating a foundation for moral behavior in teens. This is, in fact, the most important element of all. To expect moral behavior from a teenager that has no belief in God, who designed our moral code, is backward.

When faith in God moves from creed to consciousness, from mental ascent to an activated relationship, then we've moved into a realm where morality is both meaningful and possible. It's the bottom line. From that vantage point, a moral code provided by a loving, all-knowing God makes a lot more sense.

There is quite a cosmic irony when it comes to the concept of morality. God designed a moral formula to keep the fabric of human existence healthy and happy. "Keep My commandments and you will live." Amazingly, those commands for our livelihood, when carried out, also bring God joy and glory. He's happy when His creatures are happy. The heralds of moral unrestraint never point out the fact that God's laws are designed for our ultimate well-being. But if we're going to help teenagers live successfully, we'd better make this clear. When we strain at our leash, we choke ourselves.

No wonder the ultimate sin is pride, and the unforgivable sin is unresponsiveness to the Spirit of God. Independence will kill us. From the beginning of time, Satan's deception has been to convince man that independence from God's ordinances creates satisfaction. Human experience has proven that we've been tricked and lied to by the Prince of Darkness. The Bible agrees. The further we move from God's directives, the greater our losses, the larger our pain. To act in rebellion to God's principles is living hell. It will be that way for eternity.

When a sense of what is "true" and what is "right" is lost, a very real feeling of aimlessness sets in. Commenting on this, John A. Howard, former president and counselor of the Rockford Institute, wrote:

> Having spent a career trying to understand and help young people, I am convinced that the one primary cause of the tragic self-destruction of so many of our youth is that they do not know the work and satisfaction of living for something larger than themselves.
>
> The human psyche cannot stand up against moral neutrality. If nothing is truly good, right, and worth striving and sacrificing for, life is meaningless and no course of action can build a sense of one's own worth. Without larger goals, life is barren, life is a burden.[2]

The gap between a very real and loving God with a moral code and the experience of people in our culture, is an ever-widening expanse. The Christian lifestyle is based on God's absolutes and is defined with certain black and white parameters. This presents a major problem for young people. It seems like an anomaly to consider believing and abiding by moral absolutes in a society which discourages certainties. However, the Bible clearly states that certain behaviors are right and others are wrong.

Sarah wishes she could talk to you personally. If she could, she'd tell you how much she wanted some concrete standards by which to find her way through life's complicated maze. The adults in her life didn't know any, and Sarah reaped an aimless search because of it. "Adults should get a clue," she told me one day. "Kids are really confused. Of course they think they want total freedom; who doesn't? But I had total freedom and it nearly killed me. When I'm a parent, I'm going to fully teach my kids how loving God is, and why He tells us to pay attention to Him."

In order for morality to make any sense to young people, there must be an inner conviction that there is a God who created us and loves us and holds the design for abundant life. There must be a spiritual context that answers the "why's" about our behavior. Sarah just discovered that. Karen struggles with it. Gary doesn't believe it—yet.

NOTES:

1. R.C. Sproul, *In Search of Dignity* (Ventura: Gospel Light, 1983), p. 94.

2. John A. Howard, "To Quote," *Youthworker Update*, September 1989, p. 8.

GROUNDS FOR BEING GOOD

Guide Them toward Goodness

Your teen's choices may rattle you, but what you do now will have a dramatic effect on your child's perception of your values. God has entrusted you with a most challenging task—that of motivating morality in a kid who is, at the same time, submerged in a culture that is going the opposite way.

I was a pretty good kid. For the most part. Well, some of the time. There are a lot of things I did as a teenager that I wouldn't dare put in print. (Who would?) But I'll be candid about one incident that got me into a lot of trouble.

One day my best buddy, Brad, and I had some time to kill before 9:00 A.M., when school started. While walking through our little Northwest Washington town toward Vista Middle School, we passed behind a Thriftway grocery store. Now, you have to understand that the back of a large grocery store is a treasure-house of adventure for most 13-year-olds. We lived for adventure, and it seemed like an appropriate morning to dig some up.

Near the loading dock at the back of the store was a huge garbage dumpster. Its exterior had various metal ledges—serving as toeholds and handholds for us—that made for an easy climb up the approximately eight-foot high side. We swung our legs over the top of the bin and jumped in, landing in the pile of garbage, which was just a couple of feet deep. At that point it didn't occur to us that the walls on the *inside* of the dumpster were smooth. We were probably a good six feet from the top. There were no metal ledges here, and no way to climb out.

Then one of us had an even brighter idea. (I'd like to say it was Brad but I honestly don't remember.) We found a book of matches in the bin and decided we'd see if we could get a fire going. Novel idea, we thought. We fanned the little flame until it caught on. Then we added a few more scraps of paper. Great. It was going. It was going strong. It was time to put it out. We began stomping. The stomping became a little more frantic, but the fire was continuing to spread. Suddenly we hit a crucial turning point when we realized the fire was faster than we were and we just needed to get out. That's when we realized for the first time that the inside of the bin was smooth. We were about to be baked in a garbage casserole!

Our only hope was to pile some flimsy wooden crates on top of each other as fast as possible, in order to give us enough height to reach the top. That worked only so far. Then we haggled, screamed at each other actually, over who would boost whom up. The fire was raging by this time. At literally the last moment, with a lot of piling, boosting, and pulling, one of us got a leg up over the top and pulled the other up far enough to get a handhold. We jumped from the top of the bin as the fire took over inside.

For a moment we might have thought we were home free, except for the smoke billowing up heavenward. The blaze may as well have been the Goodyear blimp. In our little town it was hard to miss. In fact, someone had spotted our pyro party and called the store; the store then called the fire department, which in turn called the police. As we crossed the street, moving away from the back lot, a police car pulled up next to us. (I should say *the* police car. There was only one in town.) We'd been caught. Our parents found out. It was not a pleasant week.

How do you impart a sense of what is right and wrong to teenagers? Moreover, how do you motivate them to do what they know is right? Faith in Christ and the convicting work of the indwelling Holy Spirit is a powerful foundation. But students who don't love God, as well as those who do, still get into a lot of trouble. They skip school. They abuse alcohol. They yell at their brothers and sisters. They steal. They rebel against those who sincerely have their best in mind. They start fires.

CROSSING THE AMERICAN-MEXICAN border with a van load of teenagers is a wild experience. Supplies stuffed under seats and wedged tightly in the roof rack, we inched our way toward the immigration booth. I rolled down the window as a blast of dusty air washed in. The officer poked his head through the window and glanced at my crew. Most of them were quiet momentarily. "Where are you headed?"

"We're doing some repair work for an orphanage about an hour south of here."

"Ok," he said, motioning us on.

Just as he backed a step away from the window, Jimmy, who was sitting directly behind me, announced in a loud voice, "OK, bring out the drugs!" Everyone erupted with laughter. I couldn't bear to look at the control officer. I just hit the gas pedal while rolling up the window. Glancing in my rear-view mirror, I was prepared to see flashing lights following me, but fortunately, we slipped away without incident.

I held my speech for later. When we were stopped, I took Jimmy aside and tried to explain the poor judgment (or *no* judgment) he had exercised in his drug-related joke.

"Sorry," he confessed sincerely. "I wasn't thinking."

After an outstanding two days of ministry at the orphanage, we headed back to the border. Before crossing we gave the kids an hour to shop for trinkets in Tijuana. Little did I suspect a group of the boys had gone in search of fireworks, which, while being legal in Mexico, are very illegal in California. They knew it, too. God's smugglers. Once again we crossed the line, this time back into our home state, but with a stash of contraband burning a hole in the moral fabric of our group.

It wasn't until we got home that an informant defected out of guilt and revealed to me what most of the other students already knew. I confronted the culprits. They confessed. I confiscated the goods and we destroyed them.

The miscreants were sorry, but insisted that "everyone does it," and "no one gets caught." In the excruciating process, we talked long and hard about why things are wrong or right, about how getting away with something doesn't make it right, and about the value of respecting laws even when we may personally disagree with them. The incident was uncomfortable for all of us, but it ignited some terrific discussion and thought.

Psychologists differ widely in their understanding of how a sense of morality comes to be. Men like B.F. Skinner feel that environment is the key to development. Morality and immorality, they say, are learned behaviors, and what a kid does will determine much about who he becomes. People in good environments become good, and people in bad environments become bad.

Scholars like Piaget and Kohlberg laid the groundwork for what is referred to as the cognitive approach. This interpretation emphasizes what a person *knows*. Moral reasoning shapes behaviors, adherents claim, and moral dilemmas strengthen and raise a sense of what is right and wrong. Want improvement? Change the kid's thinking somehow.

Another strain of thought might be called the humanistic approach, which stresses each person's inherent good. According to this theory, given enough encouragement and affirmation, kids will grow up being good. Just give them time.

Finally, there is the psychoanalytic approach forged by Dr. Freud. In this system, children move from an "id" state of being (which is purely selfish) on to an "ego" state (comprehending reality), and from there the "superego" (or conscience) emerges to guide behavior. It happens rather naturally, disciples of this line of reasoning believe.[1]

All of these theories probably hold particles of truth. None of them explains the whole picture. Scripture clearly states that man is *not* inherently good. Society won't make him good. Even parental guidance isn't a guarantee. A teenager's decisions are going to reflect a composite of heredity, environment, and social interaction.

Acceptance of God's Truth is a slow process marked by experimentation, experience, and evaluation. Teenagers are developing their abilities for thinking critically. They are cracking through the shell of what they've been taught, and are experimenting with a world of conflicting ideologies. Even if faith has been nurtured during the years prior to adolescence, the journey from acceptance of parental spirituality to one of spiritual personalization is usually bumpy.

Karen is a classic example. She has grown up in a Christian home. Her dad has been a teacher and a home-Bible-study leader in our church, and I really believe that even "behind the scenes," Karen was given an environment that nurtured her faith.

But during Karen's tenth-grade year she began questioning the truths that had been instilled in her for years. Over time she became more distant, not only toward the leadership, but toward the other students in our group. She dropped out of the midweek program and only came on Sundays, quite obviously because she was expected to. Karen dressed as provocatively as possible and always sat in the back of the room. She appeared to be getting progressively more depressed.

My wife, Lori, was one of the few people who was able to stay close to Karen during this time. The two of them had great discussions about life, relationships at home, and Karen's own beliefs. She claimed over and over that her parents were stuffing religion down her throat. She felt like she was gagging. She felt she needed space to decide for herself what was real.

I wish I could say it was as easy as asking her parents to give her more space. I spoke with them repeatedly. From all I could see, her parents *were* giving her a reasonable amount of freedom. Many of Karen's indictments against her parents seemed to be purely fabricated in an effort to get Lori and I on her side.

Months went by and Karen's attitude only worsened. During this time, it became apparent she was using drugs, and when we confronted her about it, she admitted that she regularly smoked marijuana. One night Karen met with me to discuss her dislikes about our youth group, and more specifically, the hypocrites that filled it. I explained that all of our staff and students were very much in process.

During our conversation, Karen's demeanor was entirely antagonistic, and I was getting frustrated. Finally, sitting next to her on the curb of the church parking lot that evening, I blurted out, "Karen, why are you attacking everyone in your life who really loves you? You keep putting all of us down. All we've done is love you, listen to you, stick up for you, and believe in you. What are you so angry about?" I'm not sure if God's Spirit was working in Karen's heart or if I just scared her to death, but she began to cry.

"I just want to discover if God is real for *me*," Karen squeaked out between bouts with tears. "He's real for my parents, and for Lori and you, and for all these people around here. I just need to be on the other side for a while. I want to be able to look at Christianity as an outsider, so I can get perspective on it. I want to decide to follow God for myself, not just because everyone around me does."

I put my arm around her and held her as her sobs soaked my shoulder. After a long silence she calmed herself and looked at me again.

"I'll be OK. I just need some time without a lot of pressure to accept it all."

I'm sure the conversation that night did as much to change my heart as it did hers. Karen's parents were doing all they could. Now all they could do was to give her time and space.

Teenagers are like sponges. They're absorbing data from every angle. They're observing, processing, cataloging, evaluating, prioritizing, and choosing. Their perspectives change almost daily. (Have you noticed?) They're experimenting with nearly everything, to some degree, in order to mine information for themselves on every issue in question. A kind of "values basket upset" occurs. They'll screen what they see and experience through the grid of what has been modeled for them during their earlier years, and out of that process they'll develop their own set of convictions.

THE WAY THEY VIEW CHOICES

From the time children are small they are rewarded for behavior. That is all they can understand at that point. But as kids develop their reasoning capabilities, something new must kick in. We must show them by example and explanation that behavior should reflect a desire to please God who sees everything—to obey Him because He knows what will really be best for all of us in the long run.

As kids turn into adolescents, our role as adults must change. We need to become less a "director" and more of a "consultant" by the time our children are adults. The shift has to be gradual. Sudden freedom is as disastrous as no freedom at all.

I have already mentioned my wife, Lori. She does marketing consulting work on a part-time basis. As a consultant, Lori works closely with her client as a guide, creative thinker, and motivator. She helps the client to analyze the present condition, to evaluate alternatives that exist, and to internalize measures that will make the company more effective. She doesn't take over the company or demand that all of her ideas be accepted. She knows her time is limited with the client. Her goal is to help them become successful in the long range, so she works to impart a vision, to gently prod, to excite the client about change, and to kindle an inner motivation for improvement.

When it comes to moral choice-making, our role in a teenager's life is similar. Our goal is to encourage good choices independent of our control or supervision. We must instill a vision for lifelong morality that leads to genuine joy, rather than coercing choices out of fear, guilt, or some other short-term remedy. In the long run, we can work beside them but we can't force their hand.

PRINCIPLES FOR GUIDING THEM TOWARD GOODNESS

Tragically, many teenagers are caught in an "extrinsic reward" cycle. They are given strict orders, and as long as the stick-wielding authority figure is around, they'll behave. But when they are alone, or when peer pressure mounts, or when they think no one will find out, then when temptation strikes they are at a loss for owned values—they have no principles to draw on from within. Their external moral restraints—their parents, teachers, church leaders, whomever—are not around. So what happens? They fall. Moral integrity is lost, and a downward cycle is created.

So how does moral choice-making become more *intrinsically* motivated? That is, how can we facilitate the process of moving our teens toward an *inner motivation* for moral behavior? I would like to offer five suggestions. The first one begins with us as adults.

Ask yourself honestly, "Exactly what do I believe?"

Teenagers need a clearly defined value system against which to test others' values and to discover their own. When the important adults in their lives don't know what their own values are and are not sure what is right and what is wrong, what is good and what is bad, the teenager's task is even more difficult.

"My parents are always yelling at me. They say I'm lazy. 'Do your homework; clean your room; feed the cat.' But my dad just kicks back in his overstuffed chair and reads the paper after dinner. Then he says we should be having this 'family time'—that we should read the Bible together—but we never do." That's what Jimmy is observing, day after day.

Values are absorbed from what has been modeled through the constant repetition of everyday attitudes and actions. A father who cheats just a little on his income tax should hardly be surprised when he receives a notice from school that his daughter has been caught cheating on an exam. A mother who gossips on the telephone should expect her son to find no problem belittling people who don't measure up to his expectations. Words make little difference (other than to create confusion) when actions contradict what is being said.

Help teenagers to reflect and think about moral choices, beyond mere repetition of information, by teaching them to ask, "What does this information *mean?*"

The fact is, a lot of teenagers are bound to a pattern of repeating the same pat answers that got them gold stars in Sunday school, with little or no thought. Now that they have the faculties to *think* about the information they've heard, we must facilitate their doing so.

When a passage of Scripture is read, a moral stance is taken, or a social issue is discussed at dinner, the stage is perfectly set for bringing moral reasoning from the realm of principle into our tangible world. Information means little to us until we've had a chance to think it through, discuss it with others, consider conflicting opinions, and reflect on its meaning and possible implications.

Pick any passage of Scripture which touches on how we should think or act. Take Philippians 2:5-7 as an example: "Your attitude should be the same as that of Christ Jesus: Who, being in very nature God, did not consider equality with God something to be grasped, but made himself nothing, taking the very nature of a servant, being made in human likeness." That's great. But what does it *mean?* What impact did it make on Christ's way of life? What was the impact on the world? What difference would it make if we followed His example? What if we don't?

Recently, two seventh-grade "best friends" in our youth group declared all-out war on each other. Apparently one had said something slanderous to someone about the other. The maligned girl heard about it. Anger flared. Heated words were exchanged. Even the parents took sides and entered the ring. No resolve was in sight. Then came Philippians 2:5-7 to the rescue. Once we got the guilty parties to sit together and judge themselves according to God's Word, things began to change. We talked about how Christ was misunderstood. How he was slandered. How he reacted. How he forgave. After a great deal of consideration and prayer, hearts softened and tears flowed.

The relationship was restored. But only after Scripture was internalized and acted upon.

Challenge your teenagers' set patterns of thinking by asking, "*Why* do we do what we do?"

I appreciate what Chuck Swindoll had to say about this aspect of moral development:

> Training should prepare the child to think for himself. Overprotective parents, as well as easily threatened parents, are weak here. Insecure moms and dads have great difficulty inculcating solid, biblical principles in their children, apart from a long list of do's and don'ts. In many a Christian home a child is told what he may and may not do—but is not trained to understand why. That method, quite frankly, is lethal. As soon as Junior gets out of the nest (actually before) he is a ready target for the enemy's darts. His defenses are weak because he has merely learned his parents' lists. Deep within, he lacks the rationale, the conviction necessary to stand alone against a powerful world system.[2]

You remember Jimmy. His freshman year came without a lot of change. He still counted ceiling tiles. He still didn't see much of his parents. He called me one day with a question, "My parents keep saying I have to go to church. I believe in God and all that, I just don't understand why I have to attend church with them. The Bible doesn't say 'Go to church!' So why should I have to?"

Great question, I thought. So I asked him *why* his parents go to church. It took some coaching, but within minutes he'd given me a pretty complete list of benefits from gathering together with God's people. We went on to discuss examples and principles from the Word of God. I'm not sure he hung up the phone wanting to go to church. But there's one thing I am sure of: Jimmy understood *why* his parents wanted him to go. He understood the why behind the what, and that provides the basis for making wise choices.

Help them personalize moral behavior by asking, "So *what difference* does this make in my life *right now*, as well as in the future?"

Let's consider the above example again. I could have gone on to ask Jimmy how he might actually benefit from church at this point in his life, as well as down the road. With some help, his list may have included benefits such as developing a closer relationship with God, getting more of his questions answered from the Bible, making new friends, deepening close friendships, having a place for prayer and worship, having a chance to participate in exciting service projects that help others, and so on.

With these aspects of the church in mind, Jimmy would be in a better position to evaluate what difference church attendance makes. Unless he knows what difference it makes in his own experience, there is little likelihood of continued involvement.

Provide experiences which require teens to evaluate, "Am I willing to make *sacrifices* to act on what I believe to be true?"

Moral reasoning is always cemented by tough choices, by action. When experience matches with belief, the future of moral decision-making is positive. This is the case with the teenagers at Mission Hills, where I work. Because we believe in the value of unborn children, our students participate in peaceful demonstrations of that conviction. Because we believe in assisting the poor, the students travel to Mexico each year to help with building projects and to provide supplies. Because we believe that time alone with God is essential to spiritual maturity, we provide our students with devotional guides, help them learn to pray, and strive to hold them accountable for personal growth.

You get the idea. The same should be true at home. When teenagers see that our moral stance costs us, and that we're willing to pay the price, then they naturally interpret it as having value.

But a critical truth must be reckoned with in every discussion, in every dilemma, in every decision. Christ did everything right. He asked all the right questions and responded with all the right answers. He provided the perfect example in a very imperfect world. He modeled, molded, and manicured perfectly. If ever faith would flourish, it would have then. Still, some walked away. Some shook their heads and chose a different path. Christ was God and yet he allowed for individual choice. He was willing to live with that. He was even willing to die with it in mind. We need to come to terms with it as well. It has always been that way, and will always be a factor in growing toward goodness.

WANTING TO BE GOOD

In my experience with assisting teens in the difficult process of setting internal standards for moral behavior, I've found the following eight points to be helpful:

1. Teens should understand the biblical rationale behind prohibitions or expectations.

Let's say your son Chad wants to go to a party. There will be a live band and dancing. Some students might be drinking but it won't officially be allowed. Will you let him go or not? Either way you decide, there should be a solid biblical basis underlying why you feel the way you do. To say "Well, I just don't like parties," or "You shouldn't be hanging out with those people," isn't very helpful. Do a little Scripture digging with your teen before arriving at a decision—he'll see you trying to make a wise choice, not just a biased one.

What does God think of parties? Does the Bible say that dancing is right or wrong? How about drinking? You may consider verses such as these:

> "Therefore, since Christ suffered in his body, arm yourselves also with the same attitude, because he who has suffered in his body is done with sin. As a result, he does not live the rest of his earthly life for

evil human desires, but rather for the will of God. For you have spent enough time in the past doing what pagans choose to do—living in debauchery, lust, drunkenness, orgies, carousing and detestable idolatry. They think it strange that you do not plunge with them into the same flood of dissipation, and they heap abuse on you. But they will have to give account to him who is ready to judge the living and the dead" (1 Peter 4:1-5).

"You, my brothers, were called to be free. But do not use your freedom to indulge the sinful nature..." (Galatians 5:13).

"Let us behave decently, as in the daytime, not in orgies and drunkenness, not in sexual immorality and debauchery, not in dissension and jealousy" (Romans 13:13).

"...a time to mourn and a time to dance..." (Ecclesiastes 3:4).

"The Son of Man came eating and drinking and they say, 'Here is a glutton and a drunkard, a friend of tax collectors and sinners.' But wisdom is proved right by her actions" (Matthew 11:19).

"Do not join those who drink too much wine...for drunkards and gluttons become poor..." (Proverbs 23:20).

So what is God getting at? What is right? You may discuss the fact that if you're tempted to abuse drugs or alcohol, then attending a party or a dance where they are available would probably be a bad call. If you're in an environment that could intensify temptations to compromise sexually, then that too would contradict what Scripture teaches.

But consider Cindy. She has come out of a background of intense partying, and she understands the environment well.

She is sickened by the abuses that are sometimes associated with dances and certain parties. She attends parties now and then solely to influence her friends in a positive way. She dances because she loves to dance, but if a song is offensive to her faith, she won't dance to it.

I go to a couple of parties every year myself. Due to the nature of Lori's work, we are invited to cocktail parties now and then. I choose to attend because it gives me, a minister, the opportunity of building relationships with people who would never set foot in my church. I'm always shocked by how quickly conversations turn toward spiritual issues. People are shocked to find a minister out enjoying conversations with people who have no connection with a church. Some of my best opportunities to discuss the love of Jesus Christ with people have occurred in a lounge full of men and women who came to discuss business.

Attitudes, motivations, and actual behavior seem to be the focus of Scripture when it comes to an issue like partying. Still, all of us must determine through prayer and sensitivity to the Holy Spirit how we ought to decide.

2. Teens should be included in drawing up standards for conduct.

So let's say you OK his attending the party. Now the issue is one of personal character and responsibility. It's time to ask Chad how he's going to respond, especially if given opportunities to compromise on what he knows is right. How might Jesus be acting if He were at the party? What will Chad do if the party gets out of hand? Or, what will he do if those he is getting a ride with have been drinking?

3. Teens should be able to voice their opinions and be heard.

Maybe, for instance, you feel really uncomfortable with the idea of his attending the party. Based on a study of God's Word, you felt there were too many factors pointing toward a "no" on this one. Will you give Chad ample time to share his perspective, even though it differs from yours? Will you dialog with him, much as you would with another adult? Will you really strive to understand the pressure he's under to feel as though he fits in? Have you considered offering a more positive alternative (like throwing a pizza party in your own home)? Are you communicating that you understand how much he loves to dance and hang out with his friends? Those issues are as critical to most teens as your final decision.

4. Teens should be given space to exercise their own tastes and styles when these are not in conflict with God's values.

Let's say Chad gets to go to the party and he decides to wear something you hate. Have you communicated an openness to choices that don't conflict with God's standards, even though they may be different from your own preferences? Even though your tastes are completely the opposite, are you willing to give on this point in order to save your "punch" for a really critical issue?

5. Teens should know in advance what rights will be altered if they choose to act irresponsibly, and what freedoms will be granted for proving to be responsible.

As Chad leaves for the party, does he go with a clear understanding of what consequences he faces if he goes "out of bounds"? Let's say he did decide to drink at the party. Have you discussed that possibility with him, and explained where you're coming from, what the law states, and what God's Word says? Have you discussed what kind of personal discipline he would face if he chose to act irresponsibly? Have you talked with him about the freedoms you're anxious to bestow if he acts in a responsible way? Often, we fail to include this last one . . . but it's the most important of them all!

6. Teens should feel that we believe they will succeed, and even exceed our expectations on their own initiative.

For Chad to leave feeling a huge cloud of doubt surrounding him does little to evoke good choices. A much more motivating atmosphere is one of hope, belief, and positive anticipation. What if you were to give Chad a big hug and let him know that you're letting him go because you're so proud of how he had conducted himself in certain past situations?

7. Teens should receive a full measure of love and understanding, while being held to standards and repercussions that have been established.

So Chad gets home. He blew the curfew you had decided on together; he was an hour late and didn't call. Now what? Do you let it go? Do you scream and yell? Do you lay on the guilt nice and thick? Or, do you explain your concern, balancing love and firmness? He needs to know where you stand. So you decide that the next time he's out the curfew will be an hour earlier. Make it clear *why*. Make it clear that to act responsibly increases freedom, but that to shirk responsibility will only tie his hands. Also, make sure he knows you love him and believe the best regarding the future.

8. Teens should be able to internalize a freeing sense of forgiveness for failures, once they have honestly dealt with them and appropriate restitution has been made.

Guilt held over a kid's head will drive him crazy in the short run and drive him away in the long run. In Chad's case, once the discussion is over, it should really be over. He should feel as though, once he's come in on time the next time, his slate is clean. He needs to feel as though you can forget as well as forgive. It's the only way for him to visualize himself being successful in the future. To feel like a failure that cannot change is to become one.

"SOMETIMES I JUST WANT to scream," Darlene lamented over the phone. "First I told her not to leave without cleaning up her bedroom. Well, she left anyway. Then she comes in at 7:15—knowing full well we eat at 6:00 every night. I'm ready to hit the ceiling, and she just walks by, grabs a piece of chicken off the counter, and says she's going to be on the phone for a while so don't bother her.

"Well, that was it. I told her we needed to talk. But at that point I was so mad I asked her if I we could meet in 15 minutes. She said she couldn't understand why I was so upset, but agreed to meet. Then I went out into the back yard.

"I just walked around out there for a while. That's when I saw these birds. It's amazing how God gets your attention sometimes. I saw these birds just looking for food, chirping away, seemingly happy and relaxed—and then I remembered how God promises His care for us. I remembered the verse that says if He takes care of even little birds, obviously He wants to take care of us. I started to pray. I confessed my anger and asked for patience and wisdom. And Daniel, you know what?" There was a pause.

"What?" I asked, wondering what was about to unfold.

"He did. He really calmed me down. I went in and was a lot more relaxed during my talk with Karen. I also felt more confident. I explained my point of view and gave her time to explain hers. I discovered that at the last minute one of her friends came by and told her that a bunch of her best girlfriends were going over to this other girl's house right then, to surprise her on her birthday. That's why she had left without cleaning her room. I also found out she was delayed because she couldn't get a ride back as soon as she had hoped. It just hadn't occurred to her to give me a call. She apologized. But you know what?"

"What?" I countered intelligently.

"It turned out to be a really positive talk. We laid down some ground rules for the future. We worked them out together. First, if she leaves unexpectedly, she will leave a note of explanation. Second, if she gets delayed she will call, no matter what. If she doesn't, the following weekend will entail a couple of extra hours of helping me around the house. She agreed to it. I feel a lot better now.

"She still sees no point in cleaning her room, but I'm willing to flex on that. We agreed to a once-a-week cleaning. I just wanted to let you know. Sometimes I feel like giving up, and then it seems like God gives me something positive to hang on to."

Darlene and her husband are doing their best. They're working on being good examples of what they believe. They're trying to communicate with love and respect. They're trying to be wise in a thousand little ways. But Karen's world is broadening. She's reevaluating everything. She's looking for other opinions. She's opening up to other possibilities. Her world is expanding, and with that expansion comes a host of influences.

NOTES:

1. Bonnidell Clouse, *Moral Development: Perspectives in Psychology and Christian Belief* (Grand Rapids: Baker, 1985), p. 27.

2. Charles R. Swindoll, *You And Your Child* (New York: Bantam, 1980), p. 62.

MESSIN' WITH THE MIND

Help Loosen the Grip of Wrong Influences

Countless *influences are bearing down on your kid—from music and visual media to the intrigue of pornography and substance abuse. Teens face unbelievable pressures to conform. The good news is that you can help to break the grip.*

This is how Sarah described to me the role the media held in her life as a high school student, especially during her freshmen and sophomore years:

"I used to come home from school and flip on the television. Usually it was sitcom reruns. They were sort of funny, but mainly the characters argue a lot, and there's always a ton of sexual jokes. I hated soap operas but sometimes I watched them. Everybody on those things sleeps with everybody else, and they're always trying to figure out how to lie their way out of it. In the evenings my mom and I would watch TV while I'd do my homework on the floor. A lot of times my friends would call and they'd be watching the same show and we'd just talk on the phone about what we were watching, or other kinds of stuff that came up. Usually I'd watch TV till about 10 or 10:30, and then go to bed. I always go to sleep with my radio on."

As we've seen, a change of heart makes morality possible. Values are formed as we interact with God's Truth and the adults we respect. Adolescence, however, lowers the drawbridge of our lives and invites in a world of other influences. Some are healthy and some are not, but all are to one degree or another inevitable.

Lest we think our generation is waging a unique and lonely battle with the elements of evil, let's maintain a historical perspective. Evil has always abounded. Pressure to conform to the world has always squeezed hard. Cultural pressure isn't new, it's just more sophisticated. Teenagers have always faced a tantalizing array of allurements.

Boldness masking his nerves, Daniel stood to his feet. "With all due respect to your dietary rules, Sir, give us ten days. Allow my friends and me to eat what we Jews are accustomed to, and then evaluate our health after those days are up. If the others who are eating all the rich foods you offer are in better shape than us, then we will agree to eat your foods. But if not, then please allow us to eat according to our customs." Daniel sat down again. The King frowned, but agreed. It was only the beginning of conflicts to come.

Daniel was a foreigner in Babylon. Because of the Jews' own rebellion toward God, they were led away by their captors — away from their land and their lifestyle. Because of his brilliance and surprising knowledge, Daniel was among a few Jews who had been chosen to be trained for service in Nebuchadnezzar's palace. It was a rigorous three-year crash course in Chaldean life. Daniel was expected to eat their foods, apprentice under their magicians and astronomers, learn their language, and bow to their gods.

Being a teenager was hard enough. But now, to be a teenager in the court of King Nebuchadnezzar was pressure like he'd never known. While Daniel's love for God was strong, the sweet scent of a thousand different cultural spices was rising up to sweep away his attention.

Daniel's ten-day diet plan worked. He and his friends were found to be far superior in all aspects of health than those who ate the king's food. He had stood firm. He made his point. It could have cost him his life.

As time passed, King Nebuchadnezzar's ego inflated like a blimp hovering over the nation. The Jews filed in along with the throngs of Babylonians who felt obligated to worship the image. There it stood, ninety feet high by nine feet wide, encased in gold, the image that the king now called "god." Instructions were given: "When the music begins, all people are to fall and worship the image. Those who do not will be burned to death."

The music played and the people bowed, everyone but the Jews who were faithful to God. Among them were Shadrach, Meshach, and Abed-nego, and they were brought before the king. As predicted, the king's fury was aroused and the three were incinerated. But it didn't work. The Jews wouldn't burn. In fact, the whole incident was so alarming that the king fell to *his* knees and worshiped the true and living God, rather than an image made of gold.

I wish I could say the pressures to conform stopped there, but they didn't. The king's heart hardened again. Day after day Daniel faced into the blasting heat of compromise, which was designed to melt his resistance and loosen his grip. Even as he grew older and wiser, Chaldean culture continued to swoon for his love. The magnetic voice of conformity never went away. In fact, because he refused to stop praying, Daniel was thrown to the lions. Remember them? But that's another story. (See Daniel 1—3.)

David faced it too. You and I faced it. Teenagers now face social and cultural pressure like a blast of heat pouring from a hot oven. You can't miss it. You can't just ignore it; it's everywhere. One person is offering drugs. Another is talking about "getting laid." MTV is tempting and teasing and touting on a 24–hour basis. The heat is always on. The voices never go away.

Not long ago I was driving down one of our many freeways here in the L.A. area, and was stunned by an enormous billboard. It was a promotion for a morning show on one of the local radio stations. The huge ad showed Moses holding the Ten Commandments up over his head, as he did in Cecil B. De Mille's depiction of the sacred event. The caption read, "Don't Listen to Him. Listen to Kevin and Bean." The ad unfortunately reflects a voice teenagers are hearing from numerous sources.

Collectively, the media constitutes one of the most powerful sources of influence on teenagers today. Audio–visual wizardry can generate millions of fans overnight. It can take products like athletic shoes and turn them into icons. It can make the ignoble look respectable, the respectable look silly, and the sacred look insignificant. It can blast irreverent lyrics through our headsets, burst images not quickly forgotten on a 70–millimeter screen, and beam the worst behavior imaginable right into our living rooms.

From *Cosmopolitan* magazine to comedies on TV, immorality is portrayed as fun, funny, and fundamentally harmless. The portrayal is slick and glossy, and is designed to capitalize on desire. It can do that. And we buy it every day. When it comes to young people, the media shapes everything about the way they perceive the world.

THIS BEAT ROCKIN' IN MY HEAD

One verse in Romans seems to characterize much of what is being perpetrated: "Although they know God's righteous decree that those who do such things deserve death, they not only continue to do these very things but also approve of those who practice them" (Romans 1:32).

By the time you read this, any examples I offer will have become somewhat dated. So fill in your own. You won't have trouble finding material. At this writing, the music group 2 Live Crew has sold millions of albums based solely on trash appeal. Using unprintable expletives, they encourage gang rape, sodomy, and obscenities too grotesque to print.

Aimed specifically at teens are songs such as "Suicide Solution," "Necrophilia," and "Dancing in the Sheets." Rock singer Prince sings a tribute to incest in "Sister." The group Judas Priest graphically describes oral sex forced at gunpoint in their song, "Eat Me Alive." All this while teenagers ingest between three and five hours of music per day via MTV, headsets, car stereos, and radios at home. Music is at the core of the teen culture, and its influence goes beyond the beat.

Stepping into Jimmy's bedroom is like walking into an unholy sanctuary. Displayed on all four walls, as well as on the ceiling, are images of rock-and-roll heroes, bizarre otherworld creatures, and scantily dressed women in bathing suits. Peering out from one poster is a scull with blood dripping from the eye sockets. Another depicts a band member smashing his electric guitar over the head of a baby doll. What's the attraction?

"I just like the music," Jimmy explained as he laid back on his unmade bed and gazed up at the collection. "It's like an escape. I just put on my headphones and I don't have to think about all the pressures."

Leaning against the wall I thought , *That makes sense.* The music, the images, the fantasies—they all agree with our most basic sinful passions. They don't conflict with what comes most naturally. They're self–absorbing. They're sensual. They don't demand anything of us. They don't expect responsibility. They're hedonistic and rebellious. They feel good when those are the things we feel.

Al Menconi, founder and president of Menconi Ministries, which is dedicated to understanding popular music trends from a Christian perspective, explains that for teens, music is a "window to the soul." The reason popular music means so much to adolescents is that it speaks to the pains and frustrations they're feeling. Teenagers deal with feelings of anger, fear, rebellion, sexuality, powerlessness, purposelessness, depression, confusion, despair over the future of the world, and a lack of personal worth. Sound like an inventory of popular CD's? You bet. Music gives teenagers the sense that someone out there understands them and accepts them just as they are.

Right or wrong, when adults criticize the music that a teenager identifies with, it hits right at the heart. It's like someone making fun of your mother. Because they love and closely identify with their music, any attack is a personal attack, and they'll resent us for it. In most cases, depreciation of young people's music has little effect on their attitude toward that music.

It does, however, have a negative effect on their attitude toward us.

When music is viewed as a "window to the soul," much can be learned, and communication between adults and teens can be strengthened. Menconi offers some examples. Again, I must add that these examples will need to be modified with time. My goal here is that you will understand the concept. Do some research—look at current album covers, read lyrics, consider the underlying messages in their music—and supply your own examples.

A young girl's attraction to the aggressive, sexually explicit pop/dance music of artists like Madonna and Paula Abdul may reveal that she fears she'll never be attractive or loved unless she goes to similar extremes herself. The violence and rudeness of some rap and heavy-metal music by artists currently popular—such as Metallica, Megadeth, Danzig, or Ozzy Osbourne—convey the feeling of being angry and out of control. Many teenagers have good reason to feel this way.

High-flash party music by artists like Guns 'n Roses, Def Leppard, and Bon Jovi speak to the longing for a fantasy type of love, and freedom from the responsibilities and pain of life. Music by The Cure, Depeche Mode, The Smiths and Morrisey, sometimes referred to as alternative or new wave music, speaks to the attitudes of the more intellectual, introspective, and passive teen. While the music laments all that is wrong with the world, it lacks suggestions for improvement.[1]

Menconi's observations are broad and generalized, but you get the idea. Listen to what teenagers are listening to and then ask yourself, *Why?* What is in these lyrics that mirrors the inner fears and feelings of this young person? What is going on in his world that would evoke these attitudes? How can I insightfully help meet those needs, fulfill those longings, find answers to those dilemmas? Listening and loving, as opposed to lecturing, will go a long way toward helping adolescents make value judgments about the music they're digesting.

SCREEN ADDICTS

Even though one quarter of the nationwide audience for MTV is under age fifteen, everything is laid bare for viewers to marvel at—everything from rape in a gay bar to ultra-out-of-control violence. While Cher simulates sex on stage, Madonna twists fornication into a religious experience. I recently saw one of Madonna's more blatant tapes in a video store promoting "family films." As I stood watching the in-store monitor, I was flanked by four children, all under the age of ten. The five of us stood there staring at Madonna having sex on the screen. Sadly, God's gifts are being perverted and used against Him.

By the time a kid is out of high school, he'll have seen 22,000 hours of TV, 350,000 commercials, and about 18,000 televised killings.[2] Research indicates that the average teen will watch 9,230 sexual acts or innuendos that encourage sexual involvement on television every year. By the time a kid is twenty, he'll have seen more than 92,000 acts of sex or alleged acts of sex.[3] As one teen put it, "I am still a virgin and I'm glad, but I don't know how long I can hold out. Sometimes I think I'm the last one left."

Randy Alcorn, in his work, *Christians in the Wake of the Sexual Revolution,* has done an admirable job of assessing how the media has affected the moral reasoning of young people.

> One can only wonder at what premarital sexual relations are to a teenager who has seen it on TV ever since he was a preschooler? Upon finding he has fathered a child as a 16-year-old, why do his parents throw up their hands and cry, 'God, where did we go wrong?' What is the big mystery? The media has nurtured that kid on a daily diet of illicit premarital sex and taught him well that it is not only OK, but fun, funny, fulfilling, perfectly normal and generally free of consequences. The television parents use as a baby-sitter has turned out to be a kidnapper of the worst form.[4]

On January 26, 1990, the *Los Angeles Times* revealed the findings of a recent study on television violence and the toll it is taking on our sense of peace and well–being. According to the research, violence in programing aimed at young people had increased dramatically over the past three years. "For most viewers, television's mean and dangerous world tends to cultivate a sense of relative danger, mistrust, dependence and — despite its supposedly 'entertaining' nature — alienation and gloom," the report stated.[5] When rape, hatred, and every imaginable violence is piped right into the home, it is going to hurt our families profoundly.

So often we feel as though we're really helping out our teenagers by screening the super blatant stuff—the R-rated movies, the very pornographic. But the "Angel of light" doesn't need the blatant to communicate a value system. The media doesn't need to state, "Money is the new god." All it has to do is portray a success image that requires an endless array of fashion, cars, estates, and trips, while we sit drooling. It doesn't have to say, "Family relationships are worthless." It only needs to portray marriage as a trap, parents as idiots, living together outside of marriage as normal, and family communication as sarcastic and spiteful. Television doesn't usually pronounce, "There is no God." It only depicts life as if God doesn't exist—as if answers are all discovered by looking inward. Think about it. How many families portrayed in TV sitcoms go to church?

The moral climate of popular media may be at sub-zero, but as I observe the problems faced by teenagers, there are five other effects of screen addiction that should concern us. In fact, they should concern us enough to consider making one basic, radical, unpopular choice—that is, to unplug the plug–in drugs that pull us down. Let's look at these effects one at a time.

1. Decreased spontaneity
Television becomes a routine that is entirely contained in a two-foot by three-foot box. Problems set themselves up and are solved in less than an hour, without any initiative required on our part other than to sit and watch. Standardization rules out

the flaws of personal initiative. TV just isn't like real life. Once reality is confronted, we're left wanting for the ability to deal with it.

2. Lack of innovation

For those who create technology, innovation is at a high, but for the teens who saturate themselves with it, the level of innovation drops off sharply. My parents strictly limited the amount of time I was allowed to "veg" in front of the TV set. There were times I resented the controls they set. However, their consistency paid off. I became heavily involved in creating my own entertainment through building things, drawing, writing, reading, and making friends.

I often challenge the students I work with to go beyond the media for their thrills. I explain that if they're dating, to sit through a movie together doesn't do much for a budding relationship. It mandates that they simply sit down, shut up, and stare straight ahead. Besides that, many popular movies only serve to reinforce the very temptations they're trying to avoid. Every year I use one of our group times simply to help them think through all the exciting options available to them. A little brainstorming and a willingness to try something new usually results in some pretty terrific times.

3. Isolation

Most of the technology we use lulls us into becoming more self-absorbed. It reduces the need for interpersonal skills. Adults often joke about how teens today have headphones permanently attached to their ears, but in reality, it's no joke. Music drones on in magnificent stereo and blocks out the sounds of the real world and the real people around us.

Since the media don't allow for two-way interaction, they can stunt the relational maturing process. Moral growth is thwarted by a lack of involvement with people and issues. Kids can become saturated with communication that is directed right to them, with no obligation to respond to the needs of anyone else. That is hardly healthy.

4. Manipulation

Advertising controls much of our decision-making. The silver screen repetitively hammers at its agenda with bigger-than-life persuasiveness. Values are absorbed with amazing efficiency from a variety of technological sources. When the home is silent and empty, values are formed from what holds a teenager's attention.

My own experience has proven this to be so. After watching a two-hour movie in which swearing is prolific, I find myself to be much more inclined to swear. After viewing a television program which centers attention on some half-dressed blond bombshell, I admit to reminiscing about her after the program is over. If I watch a scary flick about a savage psychopathic murderer sneaking up on people, I can feel "creepy" for days. The fact is that we take in what we see. We process it mentally. Our thoughts are genuinely affected, and, unfortunately, most often in a negative way. Advertisers aren't dumb. They know media works and they're willing to bet billions on its ability to move people to action.

5. Wasted time

While technology can save time and free us up to pursue higher achievements, it generally is not used to that end. It bogs us down. Our love affair with technology has become an all-consuming relationship which prevents so much else from taking place. Students who are failing in school often describe to me the hours spent playing video games or watching TV.

Limiting the time spent absorbing what is purveyed on TV is helpful, but we must go further. We must discuss what they're seeing in light of *God's* alternative value system. We must take a stand and ask that the tube be turned *off* when what we're seeing is negative. It may be radical, but why not pray with your teen over the shows he or she watches? Ask God to give both of you the wisdom to know what's good and what's not, and to provide you with the strength to turn it off when you should.

UNDER THE INFLUENCE

Karen described to me how she began using alcohol. "The weekends were just so cool. I'd finally break free from school and my parents and all the pressures, and my friends and I would just go cruising. Sometimes we'd go to the beach and sometimes we went to someone's house, if their parents weren't home. One of my friends was over 21, so he'd buy the wine coolers or beer or whatever. I'd get pretty buzzed. It was funny. I felt so free. The rest of the week was just depressing. After a while I started sneaking some into my bedroom and drinking it at night after my parents went to bed. It helped me to not feel so bad, but it definitely made me feel lonely—you know, sitting there drinking by myself just to get a buzz."

Widespread use of drugs and alcohol has become synonymous with a description of current teen culture. In August of 1989, the Gallup organization released the results of a recent poll which revealed that more than four million thirteen- to fourteen-year-olds will have been offered illicit drugs in the past thirty days. It's not surprising, then, that the average age when kids experiment with alcohol or marijuana is twelve.[6]

Researchers estimate there are 3.3 million alcoholic teens in America. Over fifty-four percent of teens themselves say that illicit drug use among their peers is the top concern for their age group.[7] One third of our nation's high school students are problem drinkers — getting drunk more than six times per year. Consequently, America's single greatest killer of fifteen- to twenty-four-year-olds is drunk driving accidents.[8] One student explained, "Alcohol is a big problem at my high school. Every weekend, kids party. Some drink every night. The worst problem is drunk driving. I admit I have been under the influence a couple of times when driving home. Some friends of mine admit to doing it, and they brag about it. One of my friends said he was totally wasted one night and drove home anyway. He said it was like a big game to see if he could make it home."

Theories as to the "why's" behind drug use abound. Some say it helps to relieve the guilt we feel over the mess we've made of ourselves. Others say it is a natural reaction to the stresses of modern life. One thing is certain: Drugs aren't new, they've just become "normal."

The U.S. Department of Education surveyed 700 substance-abuse educators on the techniques used in teaching kids to say "No" to drugs. They were asked to rate those methods in order of preference and effectiveness. They came up with this list, in order:

- Teaching the causes and effects of drug use

- Improving kids' self-esteem

- Teaching kids to resist peer pressure

- Counseling

- Starting peer counseling programs

- Enforcing school substance-abuse rules

- Providing services for high-risk kids

- Teaching about drug laws.[8]

But even education and information aren't going to affect the inner void that has created a need in the first place. Only when God's love is applied to a kid's heart will he begin the journey toward wholeness. Only then will self-esteem find a foothold. Only then can education and information make a lasting impression.

SIMULATED SEX

"My friend's dad had a whole stack of *Playboy* magazines in his garage, and we'd go in there and look at them when his parents weren't home," one of my students wrote. "One day my friend let me take a couple of them home with me. I kept them for a couple of months and then gave them back because I felt so guilty. I still think about the pictures sometimes, and I wonder a lot about sex."

Curiosity is a normal part of sexual maturation. Pornography, however, skews the perception of what sex, as God designed it, is all about. As Josh McDowell explains so well, pornography is not wrong because it is so sexy, it is wrong because it is not sexy enough. It butchers true sexual fulfillment on the block of immediate and superficial gratification. It deprives sex of its sacred beauty and strips it of the joy that it can provide in a monogamous relationship. It sets us up for comparison, self-centeredness, and disappointment, when a real and loving sexual relationship could be ours.

It was during Randy's ninth-grade year that I got a call from Jean asking if she could come by to discuss something. Arriving in my office, I could tell she was not her usual bubbly self. Over the next few minutes she told me how she had been putting clothes away in Randy's room when she came across a pornographic magazine tucked away in the bottom of one of his drawers. Jean shifted in her chair and took a sip of coffee from her styrofoam cup. "Is this normal?" she asked. "I mean, I just don't understand how he got hold of this or why he would be into this stuff. Dennis has never had this kind of thing in the house."

Most parents don't talk to their teens about pornography. It seems too remote or too bizarre or just too embarrassing. Yet teenagers, nearly all of them, will view it before they're out of high school. Pornography in varying degrees is not relegated to adult bookstores or even racks tucked away behind counters in convenience stores. From cable TV to Calvin Klein's recent ad campaign, sexually stimulating material is pervasive. It is time to bring the issue up in our homes, because it's there whether we acknowledge it or not.

YOU CALL THESE "FRIENDS"?

Her name was Bobbie, and from the moment I brought her home my mother detected trouble. She was right. Bobbie was the love of my sophomore year. She taught me how to "make out," and gave me a very personal grand tour of female anatomy. While I was no angel, Bobbie was the epitome of everything my darker side fed on. She was really good at being bad. The values carefully seeded by years of Christian parenting were being dug up right and left. Bobbie was taunting and exciting and very persuasive.

A Minnesota Student Survey of 91,175 teenagers asked the question, "What makes you happy?" The top answer? "My friends." "My family" rated number ten on the list.[9] Adolescence introduces the peer group. To many parents they're a motley bunch. But like them or not, their influence is mammoth.

As with setting standards for goodness, underlying values are the key to helping teenagers form positive peer relationships. To say "I don't like so-and-so and I forbid you to associate with him," will probably not accomplish much. Rarely have I seen prohibitions against specific friends be very effective. What I have seen work is this: Help teenagers identify what God would want for them in their friends, what they're looking for in friends, and what kind of character qualities in others are going to fulfill those requirements.

Because my parents recognized how important my friends were to me, even those whose values were miles apart from our family's values, they spoke very carefully in their evaluations of others. What they did do was to have a brief family devotional time in the morning before we left for school. A reoccurring theme of those times in God's Word was the issue of friends. Using the book of Proverbs as a standard, rather than some criteria of their own, they helped me develop wisdom in choosing those who would influence my life. We considered and discussed verses like these:

> "The wise in heart accept commands, but a chattering fool comes to ruin. The man of integrity walks securely, but he who takes crooked paths will be found out" (10:8-9).

> "He who walks with the wise grows wise, but a companion of fools suffers harm. Misfortune pursues the

sinner, but prosperity is the reward of the righteous" (13:20-21).

"Stay away from a foolish man, for you will not find knowledge on his lips" (14:7).

"A man of many companions may come to ruin, but there is a friend who sticks closer than a brother" (18:24).

"Do not make friends with a hot-tempered man, do not associate with one easily angered, or you may learn his ways and get yourself ensnared" (22:24-25).

"Listen my son, and be wise, and keep your heart on the right path. Do not join those who drink too much wine or gorge themselves on meat, for drunkards and gluttons become poor, and drowsiness clothes them in rags" (23:19-21).

"As iron sharpens iron, so one man sharpens another" (27:17).

Bob and Janice Hunt are the parents of four children, three who are now on their own and one who is almost there. As they put it, "We had an active, noisy home—we always were busy, loud, and our home was open to anyone. We had an open fridge policy. When you came in the front door, our home was your home."

Leroy and Mary Lou Hardenbrook look back on similar memories: "We encouraged our children to bring their friends home at any time, which they did. It seems like we always had friends for dinner or staying overnight. At times we even had some of their friends go on vacation with us. We involved ourselves with their friends in the church youth group as well, helping out whenever and wherever we were needed."

There is a delicate balance between being a friend to a teenager's friends and butting out. Being there as a host, a driver, or an initiator of fun ideas can go a long way toward building better relationships. Being a positive influence is usually accepted, as long as that influence is perceived, rather than pronounced.

On the surface, most adolescents will display either disdain for our involvement or ambivalence toward it. And granted, as we have said, diplomacy and balance must be maintained. But most teens want those they love to love their friends and show it through low-key involvement.

McDonald's Corporation did a splendid job of illustrating what that looks like in a commercial that hit the media a couple of years ago. Dear ol' Dad is playing chauffeur for his young adolescent daughter and her friends. They pull up to McDonald's, and all the girls pile out and head inside. He gets out after them and his daughter turns around and says, "You're not coming in, are you?" Dad leans against the side of the car and wistfully replies, "Uh, of course not." Later on, the girl looks out through the window and sees her Dad waiting in the car. She smiles and winks at him.

OK, so it's a little sappy. But the point is well made. While an overbearing presence is resented, being there in the shadows is much appreciated.

AN EDUCATION IN VALUES

I was waiting in my car for water polo practice to finish at El Toro High School. Without warning, an unbearably loud rapping sound hit the roof of my car. I snapped my head around only to find Randy's grin pasted on the window.

Baskin-Robbins was just a mile away, and we talked about everything and nothing until we got there. Ice cream cones in hand, Randy and I walked along a row of mini-mall shops. A common story unfolded. "I wrote a paper for my senior ethics class about how all of us have a built-in sense of morality. I also wrote that universal moral beliefs are one evidence for a God who set up a moral system. You know, like we've talked about in the Student Gathering."

I couldn't remember the exact discussion but I got the idea. "Well, anyhow, Mr. Penner mentioned my paper in class and asked if I'd like to defend my position in front of everyone. I said I wasn't sure if I could. He sort of laughed and said that of course I couldn't. He said morality is just made up by society to keep it from going off the deep end. Well, I think this dude's off the wall. I know God exists."

During the next couple of hours Randy and I talked about the evidences for God. We talked about His moral blueprint that is spelled out in Scripture. And we talked about the consequences accompanying both options faced by humanity—ignoring God's Word or living by it. Despite our conversation, Randy is submerged in a school system that is spinning for lack of foundation and the ride is making most kids dizzy.

Is there really such a thing as "value-free" education in public schools? Is it even possible to educate without influencing values? Quite obviously, no. We all have values, every one of us, and virtually everything about how we relate, communicate, and educate will be affected by what we believe is true and important.

While public education attempts to restrict those who voice the values of their faith, the same just isn't true for those who voice their values because of no faith at all. Education, by its very definition, "is an enterprise in preparing people for a future. To do this, someone has to guess what that future holds and what is the best way to prepare for it. Those guesses constitute values." Dr. Cliff Schimmels, a professor of education at Wheaton College, goes on to say:

> Just the structure of the school day teaches certain values . . . Teachers make hundreds of value judgments every day. They decide which piece of material gets three days of emphasis and which piece gets only one day. They decide what they'll explain and what they won't explain. They decide what is a good piece of work and deserves an A. Conversely, they decide what isn't a good piece of work and gets a D.[10]

Naturally, this brings up an interesting dilemma. Since so much of what goes on in the public educational system conflicts with Judeo-Christian thinking, wouldn't it be better to get kids out of there, if possible? Wouldn't a Christian school environment be more conducive to nurturing Christian values and behavior? In some cases that may be true.

Some friends of Jimmy's parents suggested a Christian school for him. His grades were getting worse and he'd been in a couple of fights. Soon his parents came to the conclusion that if Jimmy were put into a Christian school, his world might be a little more stable—a little more manageable. Jimmy entered South Coast Christian in his sophomore year. It seemed to help. The loneliness and abandonment he felt from his parents appeared to be softened by a more nurturing environment with increased personal attention.

For others, a Christian school setting only makes them spiritually lethargic. As one students explained, "I've been in a Christian school all my life. Most of the kids there party more than the kids from the public schools. Most of them know all the answers but deep down they really don't care about God at all. They just want to get out. I had some friends that graduated last year. I don't think any of them go to church anymore, now that they're away from home."

Often Christians on "secular" campuses are morally stronger than Christians who have been cradled in a Christian environment. How can that be? I believe the answer to that perplexing question lies in an illustration. The story goes like this:

Many years ago, when cod was first transported from Atlantic waters to consumers on the West Coast, the fish arrived at their destination in poor condition. They tasted mushy instead of fresh. Numerous techniques were employed to resolve the problem, including shipping them alive in tanks of their own water. Still no luck. Finally, it was discovered that by putting another type of fish, a natural predator, in the tank, the cod "came to life," so to speak, and remained fresh all the way to the West Coast.

Friction induces something almost magical. When our faith is confronted, when values are questioned, when ethics are tested, refinement often follows. Like an isometric physical workout, opposing force builds strength and endurance. Without challenge, passivity quickly sets in. Morality grows soft.

Christian educators must realize the importance of teaching students *how* to think, not just *what* to think. The same thing should be happening in Christian homes, Christian youth groups, and Christian youth organizations. Projects which push Christian students out of "the Christian bubble" and require interaction with other environments, ignite a fresh disequilibrium, leading to strength.

But to be sure, the secular campus will continue to be a source of conflicting ideologies. Teenagers will face increasing opposition if they choose to stand for a belief in God and a respect for His Word.

Ron and Betty Rouland said, "We tried to teach our sons early on that they would be standing alone for Christ in their school environment and we would be there to support them and help them find alternatives to the teaching and assignments they were getting from their teachers."

Our job, then, must be to support them well and to give them tools for expressing what they believe and why in an intellectually challenging format.

One family at our church maintains a weekly family forum on Tuesday nights. After dinner they get together for an hour or so just to "rap" about an issue. Evolution, pre-marital sex, stealing, abortion, creativity, friends, homosexuality, greed. You name it, they talk about it. At each family gathering, the kids choose the following week's topic. Dad and mom do some research on the issue. When they all get together on Tuesday, not only do they have a lively discussion but the kids discover what the varying viewpoints are. They learn how to approach difficult issues, how to share and defend their positions, and where to go to find resources and answers. It's a great idea that *works.*

NOTES:

1. Al Menconi with Dave Hart, "Talking 'Bout the Way I Feel . . . .," *Christian Parenting Today*, April 1990, pp. 25-27.

2. Stewart Powell, "What Entertainers Are Doing to Your Kids," *U.S. News and World Report*, 28 October 1985, p. 46.

3. Josh McDowell, *What I Wish My Parents Knew about My Sexuality*, (San Bernardino, Calif.: Here's Life Publishers, 1987), p. 43.

4. Randy Alcorn, *Christians in the Wake of the Sexual Revolution*, (Portland: Multnomah Press, 1985), p. 103.

5. *Los Angeles Times*, 26 January 1990, sec. F, p. 1.

6. Vic Sussman, "News You Can Use," *U.S. News and World Report*, 11 September 1989, pp. 70-72.

7. Jolene L. Roehlkepartain, "15 Going on 35," *Group*, April/May 1990, pp. 14-15.

8. Kevin Leman, *Smart Kids, Stupid Choices*, (Ventura: Gospel Light Publications, 1982), p. 130.

9. "News, Trends and Tips," *Group*, April/May 1990, p. 11.

10. Cliff Schimmels, "Questions Parents Ask about Schools," *Focus on the Family*, March 1990, p. 21.

WHEN HELL BREAKS LOOSE

Make Your Home a Teenager's Haven in a Crazy World

Even during adolescence, what happens at home and within the family has more to do with a kid's decisions than anything else does. In a turbulent world, the home can be a teenager's primary source of strength.

Sarah painted a more desperate picture of the past than I had imagined. "When my dad left home I was devastated. Every few days my mom would get in a really bad mood and slam my dad for all the things he did wrong in their relationship. I used to sit at the dining room table and listen to her until I couldn't take it anymore. A lot of times she would apologize to me the next day, but nothing really changed. I would always think to myself, *So what does this have to do with me?* I really loved my dad.

"Mom began drinking every night when she got home from her nursing job. Sometimes she had dates and then she would be really happy for a few days. A few of the guys she dated lived with us for a while. Lived with her, I should say. I thought they were just using her. I really resented the fact that she wouldn't let me visit my dad. She always said he would 'corrupt' me, but inside I felt like *she* was the one corrupting me.

"One night I was watching TV and this guy that was staying in our apartment was there. My mom was on her shift at the hospital. I think I was about eleven years old, but I don't remember for sure. Anyway, he started putting his hands all over me. I said I was afraid my mom would come home—to get him to stop. It didn't phase him. He just kept holding on to me and touching me everywhere, even though I was trying to get away.

"I really don't even remember everything that happened. It's all sort of a blur. I just know I hated it. I remember afterward wishing that this guy was my dad because I wanted so much for my dad to love me. It sounds really strange, but I remember thinking that."

Sarah talked for more than an hour about her experiences at home during junior high. I asked her if her mother ever found out about any of it. "Are you kidding? My mom would have thought I was lying. I would have died of embarrassment to talk about it. Besides, she was so totally into her own problems. I didn't want to burden her with mine."

I believe Sarah left my office that day feeling some of her emotional baggage had, at least for a moment, been lifted from her shoulders. The weight *I* felt seemed heavier than ever. I drove home feeling so deeply sad for the thousands of Sarahs who live the nightmare every day. Sarah's is an extreme case. But things are not well in many of our homes. The private lives of those who lead, teach, and parent America's teenagers are increasingly being classified as "dysfunctional."

On Monday morning, February 19, 1990, I stumbled out onto our front porch and retrieved the *Los Angeles Times*. Clearing the sleep out of my eyes, I focused on a headline that read, "Sex, American Style: Trend to the Traditional." I thought, "Hey, this ought to be a fresh twist." Then I read the article which revealed the findings from a recent, fairly extensive survey of American sexual standards. It reported that the average American adult has had more than seven sexual partners. The average divorced adult has been to bed with more than thirteen different people!

Moreover, the study showed that about 70 percent of married men have had at least one sexual partner in addition to their wife during their marriage, and 35 percent of the married women had been to bed with another man at some point. I shook my head. The article was ironically supposed to show that we as a people are not nearly as promiscuous as the researchers had thought.[1]

Back in 1969, 68 percent of the general public felt that premarital sex was wrong. By 1973, just four years later, only 48 percent believed it was wrong. By 1985, *U.S. News and World Report* showed that the figure had dropped to a mere 36 percent of the population in general. However, of people between the ages of 30 and 44 (many of whom are parents of teens), only 25 percent felt that sex prior to marriage was wrong![2]

And the effect of this modeling on teens? According to figures released by the U.S. Center for Disease Control in early 1992, teenagers are heavily into sexual relationships. Among ninth-graders, 40 percent have had sex already. By tenth grade the figure jumps to 48 percent. By their junior year, 57 percent have become sexually active. And by the time they're seniors, 72 percent, nearly three quarters of all teens, will have already lost their virginity.[3] Another report indicates that 30,000 thirteen- to fourteen-year-old girls become pregnant each year.[4]

WE MUST STAY CLOSE TO THEM!

Teenagers are looking for love. They long for closeness. In fact, they're desperate to find it. They're convinced love must find its zenith in sex, so they throw their virginity to the wind in hopes of catching something that will fill their hearts. While few are catching love, many are catching diseases.

In one day in America, over 33,000 people will contract a sexually transmitted disease. That's twelve million people per year! Many of these will be teens. Tragically, thousands of them will be contracting AIDS.[5] While it is impossible to keep up with escalating rates of diseases, it's a widely accepted fact that AIDS has now been detected in more than a million Americans, and has claimed the lives of thousands of them. Its spread is epidemic and is now hitting teenagers in an unprecedented way.

On Christmas Eve my wife, Lori, and I sat in a second-row pew at our church, waiting for the service to begin. The whole scene was festive and the thrill of Christmas hung in the air. Directly in front of us sat a young man in a wheelchair. He was slightly hunched over and leaning to one side, and looked to be in his early twenties. Neither Lori nor I knew who he was, and I had every intention of introducing myself after the service. As was the case, however, my attention was drawn another direction as soon as the service was finished, and I didn't have a chance to talk to the man.

Later on that week, I asked our senior pastor if he knew the man. He did. This guy, I discovered, had been a practicing homosexual, was barely out of his teens, and was now dying of AIDS. Suddenly the reality of a frightening killer had visited *my* world. Jim died soon after that Christmas, but the memory of his crumpled frame sitting in front of us stands as a memorial to the plight of our age.

No matter which statistics you rely on, all of them conclude that more than half of our teens, by the time they're out of high school, have already had sex with someone outside of marriage. Also well-known is the fact that one of the fundamental reasons teens are becoming sexually involved so soon is their longing to be loved and held.

In an article entitled "The Lives of Teenage Mothers," published in the April 1989 edition of *Harper's Magazine,* one cure for the intimacy drought is to create a new family, one that it is hoped will offer the love that has been missing. The author writes, "Part of the motivation for teenage girls to have babies is a wish to be reborn themselves, to re-create themselves as children, so they can get the love and attention they feel they were denied.[6]

"When I was fifteen, my mom remarried," Sarah explained. "I liked the guy, more or less. He was pretty nice to me but I still wanted to visit my dad, which my mom wouldn't let me do.

"It was during that year that I got pregnant. This guy—his name was Darrel—and I had been dating for a long time . . .

like five or six months. We were really close. We started sleeping together, and we talked a lot about running away. He was 19 and said that as soon as he could get the money together we would move out and live together. It was like all I wanted." Sarah's eyes welled with tears.

"I wanted someone to love me so bad." Sarah paused for a minute. "Then I started thinking about this baby. At first I was really excited, like I could give it a better life than I had. I thought about holding it, and how it would love me. Then I'd get really freaked out and start thinking about how I was going to make a living and everything. What's weird is that Darrel started acting really different. He started avoiding me. It was like we were breaking apart. I knew then that I had to get an abortion. There was no way I could deal with this."

Over the years I have known a number of teenage girls who have become pregnant out of wedlock. In nearly every case, these girls have felt deprived of emotional support. They were, in effect, searching for someone who would affirm their worth.

I've made an example of our shift in sexual standards, but this is only one of countless issues that confront our families. Values of all sorts are absorbed from those who have the greatest influence over us. Various authority figures, people we idolize, the educational system, mass media, and peer relationships, all contribute to the formation of values. They all model behaviors for our kids. While each of these has influence, the strongest teacher, even during adolescence, is what teens see in the adults they're closest to—their parents.

Randy is pretty typical. Sometimes he resists even the best events planned by his parents. He doesn't like them lecturing. He tests the limits of his relationship with them. He tells them they can't relate. But despite all of that, he'd tell you he respects them. He knows they really care for him, and he believes that most of what they say is right. "I just don't want to hear it sometimes. I just want to be able to make my own choices." He laughs. "But I know they're usually right. I know they'd do what they're telling me to do."

Recently a study was conducted in Sweden in an effort to determine what type of environment was contributing to an upsurge in teen delinquency there. Surprisingly, the researchers found that the teens who were most undisciplined did not necessarily come from undisciplined or troubled homes. A disproportionate number of these kids came from homes where the parents simply did not *practice* the kind of lifestyles that they demanded of their adolescents. The students who appeared to be well behaved came from homes where the parents *lived* the lifestyle they expected of their children.[7]

Ron and Bette Rouland have four boys, now all in their twenties. All of them are walking with God and striving to serve Him with their lives. "Bette and I realized very early on, it's not what we teach by words that counts, but by living it out first in our own lives. All of our sons agreed that this was what made the greatest impact in their lives."

As Paul was readying to send Timothy to the church in Corinth, he wrote of Timothy: "He will remind you of my way of life in Christ Jesus, which agrees with what I teach everywhere in every church" (1 Corinthians 4:17).

In his words to the believers in Thessalonica, he reiterated the same integrity: "For we know, brothers loved by God, that he has chosen you, because our gospel came to you not simply with words, but also with power, with the Holy Spirit and with deep conviction. You know how we lived among you for your sake. You became imitators of us and of the Lord; in spite of severe suffering, you welcomed the message with the joy given by the Holy Spirit. And so you became a model to all the believers in Macedonia and Achaia" (1 Thessalonians 1:4-7).

And did you happen to notice the outcome? They became imitators of Paul. Not because of his *lectures* but because of his *lifestyle*. Unless the Truth has gotten through to us to the point that our actions match our words, how can we be trusted? Do we have any right to expect teenagers to trust what we say if our life contradicts it? Although teenagers are not as open to being told what to do and think, they are more open than ever to being shown. What the adults in their lives do or don't do is still the primary influence.

We really do want to be models of unity, love, faithfulness, and all the qualities that make families safe and functional. But how does effective modeling work? How do we take what is good and pass it on to them? It begins with *openness*.

When adults who are close to teenagers open up their lives, when they're authentic and honest, teenagers are interested. Writing to parents of teens, Psychologist Earl Wilson notes:

> Teenagers do care what you believe, and they care deeply. They just aren't going to swallow it whole without chewing and tasting it for a while. They want you to share your values with them because your value system is the only value system they are able to scrutinize in depth. They observe what others believe and how they live, but not at the same depth that they look at the life you have chosen.[8]

And the encouraging news is this: By the time most young people reach their mid-twenties, their moral convictions nearly match those displayed by their parents or their other adult role models. Dr. James Dobson surveyed 853 parents and found that of their then rebellious children, now grown, 53 percent accept their parents' values, 32 percent somewhat accept their parent's values, and only 15 percent said they still rejected the values modeled by their parents.[9] Our major concern should be, not to get teens to act the way we want, but rather to act that way ourselves. Then, when our teens become like us, we will like who they are!

CARTER PSYCHIATRIC HOSPITAL IS a tense place. That's where Gary and I met again. The night he and his gang friends cornered Larry Jensen, I suspected Gary was headed for trouble. And on the night I helped hold him down on the concrete driveway of his home, I *knew* he was in it—deep.

After being admitted past the locked entry, I headed down the ammonia-scented corridor toward Gary's room. I knocked, and a moment later the door opened. Standing there was a thin kid with long, greasy bangs covering his eyes. "Yeah?" he asked, matter-of-factly.

"Is this Gary's room?" I inquired. He pushed the door open all the way and stood to the side. Gary was lying on a bed across the room; he had headphones on. "Hi, Gary." He just nodded. "What's your name?" I asked Gary's roommate.

"That's Eric," Gary loudly interrupted, before Eric could answer for himself. Eric walked out the open door without a word. It slammed hard behind him.

I sat on the bed across from Gary and attempted a conversation, despite the headphones which remained in place. "So how's it going?" I asked.

"It's OK."

"Really?"

"Actually, I hate this d - - - - - place."

That was the beginning of the next half hour. It was mostly one-sided. Gary wasn't in much of a mood to talk. When he did talk his words were filled with anger toward his mom and dad.

"They act like they think they're religious or something. It's like they show up at church now and then just to impress you guys. At home they're total hypocrites. Every time anything goes wrong, my dad takes out all his anger on me. He hits me and s - - - like that. I want to get out of here, but I'm not going home if I can help it."

"Why's that?" I asked.

"Like, I'm sure I want to get beat up on all the time. One time he broke one of my ribs and I had to go to emergency just to make sure I was OK. Someday I'm going to come back and kick his butt."

As I drove down the winding drive leading away from Carter Hospital, I could only speculate on what kind of inconsistencies may have contributed to Gary's situation. What happens at home is like a megaphone next to a teenager's ears. Sure there are other voices. Just none so loud. None so clear.

THE SILENT REMINDER OF WORTHLESSNESS

While the national debate rages over the abortion issue, there is one angle that doesn't get much attention, if any. No one is talking about what abortion communicates to the living—to those who have slipped past the abortionist's scalpel. Or to those who know that millions of their brothers and sisters are annihilated each year. No one is talking about what this is doing to the teens who know they're living in a society that has sanctioned the slaughter; and to those who know that it's mothers and fathers like their own who are killing their babies. Do you think this impacts teenagers?

One of my students wrote the following: "I was born in 1973, the year abortion became legal. It blows me away to realize I could have been slaughtered because of a slight birth defect (my left arm doesn't work right). I'm only glad my parents loved me anyway. Obviously, not all parents do. That is frightening."

I firmly believe that both the people who abort and the children who are aborted are victims of a profound misunderstanding about the value of life. And teenagers are judging their own worth against the backdrop of this reality.

THE MONSTER IN THE HALLS OF OUR HOMES

A child psychologist at the University of Texas has made a strong claim: "Sexual abuse, and especially within the family unit, will be the crime of the 90s." He added that the incidence of sexual abuse in this country is "staggering."[10]

A good friend of mine, Mike, who is a music minister in our area, found himself constantly beset by one physical illness after another. His right shoulder, greatly taxed in the process of conducting music, was creating pain so intense that he was unable to carry out his duties as choir director and pianist. Finally, he was hospitalized and underwent more than one painful operation.

Mike's physical problems dragged on for nearly a year, until his discouragement gradually melted into a severe depression. Then, after numerous tests and various therapies, Mike was admitted to a psychiatric in-patient facility.

In time, Mike was back leading music in his church, and over the months that followed it appeared that his physical problems were also improving. The entire episode had been bewildering to a congregation that loved him deeply and had stood by him throughout the entire ordeal. One Sunday morning my wife attended the service where Mike told his church family about some of what he had discovered during his psychiatric treatment.

As a child Mike had endured numerous family problems, and had trusted in the friendship of his family's doctor. As it turned out, the doctor had sexually molested Mike to the extent that emotional wounds still festered, threatening to wreck his health, his family, and his career—thirty years later!

Mike's experience is hardly an isolated incident. In our own church we now have a support group solely for women who were sexually abused as children.

Samuel Nigro, writing in the November 21, 1988 issue of *U.S. News and World Report*, put it succinctly when he said:

> **What is done to children is an outrage. They are aborted, deprived of real mothers, savaged with electronic baby-sitters, filled with violence and disgust, surfeited with active and passive pornography. We institutionalize their abuse and educate them into spiritless sociopaths—all for the grandiose gratification of pompous adults and their arrogant misunderstanding of rights that are massively bereft of truth, love, and thought. [11]**

Given the world that exists, we who are concerned for children and teens must do anything in our power to reestablish safety in our families. It may mean becoming more informed through agencies like Focus on the Family, or getting professional help, or assisting with a political campaign. Both our attitudes and our actions on issues such as child abuse and abortion communicate volumes to the next generation.

HARMONY WHERE IT COUNTS THE MOST

American families face another enormous problem. In 1870, only one marriage in thirty-four ended in divorce. Two generations ago, the divorce rate had risen to one in twelve. In the last generation it was up to one in three, and at present some researchers place the divorce rate at about half of all marriages![12] A 1986 poll among Christian youth workers indicated that in any group of adolescents, between thirty-five and seventy-five percent will not be living with both of their natural parents.[13] Children who grow to adulthood in the traditionally defined nuclear family are now in the minority.

Many kids today have lost the sense of well-being that comes from stability in the family. A child's home is no longer an oasis in a crazy world. The craziness has come right through the front door, with so much force that families are breaking apart at the rate of one every twenty-seven seconds.[14]

A great deal of research has gone into determining what effect separation and divorce has on kids as they grow older. One study, conducted at Indiana University, found that among males, those whose parents had been divorced before they were two years of age were more willing to try coercive tactics to have sex. Girls with divorced parents, the study found, were more aggressive and sexually active, while guys from those homes favored recreational sex over committed relationships.[15]

Sadly, however, our staggering divorce rate is only one indicator of the trauma. Many families in which both parents are *present* have become emotionally hollowed out. Without generalizing to an extreme, it's safe to say that behind many deeply troubled teenagers lies a backdrop of conflicts at home.

A strong marriage is an incredibly powerful influence. It's the foundation of a family. It's the children's principal model for love. It's the enduring example of unity and safety in a world rife with hatred, betrayal, and selfishness. But a marriage gone bad, whether it breaks up or not, is an equally powerful force. Just ask the kid who is going through it. He's the innocent victim, the one who can't help but sense some blame, the one who has no control but must endure all of the confusion.

As one kid in our youth group recently told me: "I'm moving out as soon as I can. I'm sick of living with constant fighting between my mom and dad. I think maybe if I got out of there, things would be better."

All of this reveals one overarching truth: Marriage is worth the work. It may mean drastically restructuring priorities. It may mean changing a job or curtailing some personal interest. It may even require the time and expense of counseling. But the sacrifices pay off. Studies conducted with early adolescent students reveal the value of a home where harmony reigns:

> **Adolescents in a close family unit are the ones most likely to say "no" to drug use, premarital sexual activity, and other antisocial and alienating behaviors. They are also the ones most likely to adopt high moral standards, develop the ability to make and keep friends, embrace a religious faith, and involve themselves in helping activities.[16]**

Joe and Mary Merwin, the parents of three children now in their thirties, told me: "The strongest statement you can make to your teens is a united front and a oneness of mind in your marriage. You must expect failure in yourself, your mate and your children. But, you can use that failure to grow in patience and in your dependence on Christ."

I'm well aware that many who read these pages are single parents. The good news is that God isn't limited to the past. Nearly every week I hear of husbands and wives, as well as single moms and dads, who are taking steps to change the way things are. Let me share with you a few important steps that are critical to shaping the future.

First, *we must turn our difficulties over to God.* In a very real sense, we must be willing to go to Him *first*, pour out our hearts in prayer, and begin to immerse ourselves in his Word. Whether or not we're aware of it, God is as hurt by our sufferings as we are. He's also powerful, and willing to answer our prayers. But first we must humble ourselves and seek Him by faith.

Second, *we must begin with ourselves.* As much we may wish our spouse would change, this change is generally beyond our control. What we *can* do is evaluate the situation and determine how we personally can improve the relationship. Single parents must be willing to ask themselves the tough question, "Am I doing all I can *now* to provide an example of love, forgiveness, and stability, despite the past?"

Third, *we must be willing to seek help.* Nothing is more self-defeating than attempting to change long-entrenched patterns of relating without outside assistance. Whether it is a wise and objective friend, a pastor we're close to, or a professional counselor we are referred to, we need the perspective and objectivity of someone who genuinely cares for us.

Finally, *we must attempt to provide consistent examples of Christ and a sense of hope for our teens.* Many times this is through a church youth group, or a friend who has developed rapport with our teenager. In our group at Mission Hills, many teenagers from single parent homes find a great deal of support and direction through relationships they develop with our adult staff.

One family I counseled allowed their daughter to spend a year living with a close Christian relative in another state. The parents then spent the year going through a process of professional counseling, which strengthened their marriage. While their problems haven't vanished, they are reunited with their daughter and have a marital relationship that is stronger than ever. They are better equipped than in the past to cope with the demands of raising and loving their teen, but it required some major adjustments in how they were relating.

Creating a harmonious home environment is neither quick nor easy. As Tim Kimmel wisely writes:

> It takes a lot of courage to submit to one another, to put our partner's best interests ahead of our own.

It takes a lot of courage to work through conflict with the goal of resolution and reconciliation.

It takes a lot of courage to stand against the cultural attitudes that view marriage as tedious.

It takes a lot of courage to take the time to plot out the goals and objectives for your family that will allow you to leave a legacy of love.

It takes a lot of courage to stick with your strategy.

It takes a lot of courage to risk turning your back on influence, power, and money when those things undermine your commitment to the home.

It takes a lot of courage to be transparent—to submit your laughter, tears, hopes, and dreams to another person.[17]

Marital harmony plays such an important role in this whole issue of training teens to love God. Our obligation is to honestly assess what we can do and then take action to improve what can be changed—in order to make the home a safe haven.

HARBOR FROM HARSHNESS

As much as any time during childhood, teenagers desperately need a harbor. They need a place of safety and love, a retreat from the harshness of all they are experiencing. Kids today are facing adult-size issues much earlier than ever before in history. At age ten they're getting drunk. By eleven, many have ulcers. At age twelve some are pressured to be sexually involved. By the time they're thirteen, teens are getting high, and by fourteen they're sometimes out getting a job.

Even physical maturation has accelerated. In the early 1800s, a girl could expect her menstrual cycle to kick in at about age sixteen. Today most girls have their first period by the time they're thirteen. Ten- to twelve-year-olds are having to face some incredible dilemmas without the maturity necessary to make wise choices. Some of those decisions will impact their entire life.

The home is their last hope for reprieve and reassurance. When it, too, becomes a place of turbulence, many teens aren't able to cope.

Gary's stint in the care facility was short-lived, and nothing seemed to have changed much. Every week a man dropped Gary off at seven for our Wednesday evening Student Gathering. By nine, Gary had generally alienated nearly everyone at church. He teased other guys, verbally harassed the girls, and completely disregarded attempts by our team of leaders to encourage better behavior.

On numerous occasions I pulled Gary aside and tried to talk to him about the problems. He appeared somewhat remorseful, but by the following week (sometimes within the following hour), he would be in trouble again.

One night I saw Gary arrive and I went over and greeted him. Within fifteen minutes or so, however, he was nowhere in sight. I asked a couple of leaders if they'd seen him leave. No one had seen him at all. Later in the evening, as students were moving from one part of the building to another, an egg came flying overhead and smashed against the wall of the building. I wasn't far behind the students, and before I could detect the source, BAM! Another egg hit the building. I ran out into the parking lot. Dashing from behind a car parked next to the street, a dark figure took off running.

Our chase lasted less than a minute. At the street corner, I caught the culprit. The street light overhead revealed it was Gary. After a brief exchange that didn't seem to get anywhere, I took him with me into the church office and called his father, Vince. From all I could tell, Gary didn't seem to care. Within minutes his dad arrived. He was a large, disheveled-looking man who had the smell of alcohol thick about him. He didn't even look at Gary. The three of us walked into my office where I explained the situation.

Over the next twenty minutes I heard Vince's version of Gary's life. According to Vince, Gary's mother was "psychotic," so their divorce was just as well. Gary had an older sister who was, in the words of his father, "no problem to nobody." Both kids had lived with their mom until she remarried but were unable to get along with their stepfather; so they had moved back in with their dad and the woman he had since married.

Gary just sat staring out the window as his father proceeded to unload the boy's faults. He had been caught stealing. He was suspected of using drugs. He was always lying. He was messy and ungrateful and "a waste of time," as his father put it. He had been expelled from two different high schools in the area. He was now on probation at the third.

With every indictment I felt like a dagger was being twisted in Gary's back. He showed no emotion whatsoever. As his father's words continued, I could feel the cracking of a wounded soul.

Teenagers need to hear the good more than the bad. Even if they fail us, we need to quickly move beyond their mistakes and reestablish a positive stance toward them. Affirmation through verbal and appropriate physical expression will help build a balanced self-esteem in our teens.

HAVE YOU HUGGED YOUR KIDS TODAY?

There is an amazing psychological impact in the human touch. When a person is hugged, the level of hemoglobin in that person's bloodstream actually increases. Hemoglobin supplies the brain, heart, and other organs with oxygen. Experts tell us that an increase in hemoglobin affects our total health. It helps to prevent disease and contributes to recovery from illness. Hugging has been shown to curb harmful depression and stimulate a person's will to live.[18]

As Jimmy and I talked about his dad, one thing became clearer: Robert deeply loved his son. He just hadn't spent a lot of time expressing it in ways that Jimmy could understand. "Does your dad ever hug you or tell you how much he loves you?" I asked in one of our discussions.

"Heck no! My dad never hugs me. He says guys that hug each other are queers. He would never hug another guy." He paused. I waited. "I don't know; he never hugs my mom or my sister, either."

At times a teenager's drive to be secure and independent will lead him to act as though he doesn't want or need affection. And tragically, some teens already feel so unloved and ugly that they shun a personal touch. But when timed just right (usually not in front of other people) and given as an expression of true affirmation, a hug or an arm around the shoulder will slice through distance like nothing else can.

In dysfunctional, inharmonious homes, words about God and instructions for godliness are going be drowned out by the static of disunity. Unless teenagers see our values and convictions mandating the course of our own families, words and admonitions will evaporate as soon as they are spoken. Until our homes become the primary sanctuary for the incubation of all that is spiritual, teenagers will continue to move their hearts away from home and look for solutions somewhere else.

Over the years I've spoken with countless moms and dads whose children are now grown. On numerous occasions I've asked them what they would do differently, if anything. None of them have ever said they wished they had worked longer hours. None have said they wished they had been richer. None have looked back and longed for more status in their careers.

Rather, these parents have said that if they could do one thing over, they would have worked harder at building a happy home. They would have contributed more time to their marriages, to the lives of their children, and to the issues of parenting. They would have enjoyed their kids more. They would have played more. They would have laughed more. I believe that communicates a lot to those of us still in the trenches.

What will you and I say when we look back? Will we like what we see? What will our children say when they are older and look back? Will they see us, despite our flaws, having been deeply involved in the stuff of their lives? We need to prayerfully determine goals for our home and family life, and do everything we can to meet those goals—today.

NOTES:

1. Thomas H. Maugh II, "Sex, American Style: Trend to the Traditional," *Los Angeles Times*, 19 February 1990, sec. 1A, p. 1.

2. Ronald L. Koteskey, *Understanding Adolescence* (Wheaton: Scripture Press, 1987), p. 100.

3. Reported in the *Los Angeles Times*, Jan. 4, 1992.

4. Kevin Leman, *Smart Kids, Stupid Choices* (Ventura: Gospel Light Publications, 1982), p. 82.

5. Josh McDowell, *What I Wish My Parents Knew about My Sexuality* (San Bernardino, Calif.: Here's Life Publishers, 1987), 43.

6. Elizabeth Marek, "The Lives of Teenage Mothers," *Harper's*, April 1989, p. 56.

7. Ross Campbell, M.D., *Kids Who Follow, Kids Who Don't* (Wheaton: Scripture Press, 1987), p. 84.

8. Earl D. Wilson, *Try Being a Teenager* (Portland: Multnomah Press, 1982), p. 77.

9. James Dobson, *Parenting Isn't for Cowards* (Waco: Word, 1987), p. 49.

10. "USA at a Glance: Child Abuse," *USA Today*, 29 September 1989, p.1.

11. Samuel Nigro, *U.S. News and World Report*, 21 November 1988, p. 8.

12. Paul W. Swets, *How to Talk So Your Teenager Will Listen* (Waco: Word Books, 1988), p. 172.

13. Mike Yaconelli and Jim Burns, *High School Ministry* (Grand Rapids: Zondervan, 1986), p. 17.

14. Ibid., p. 17.

15. "News, Trends and Tips," *Group*, March 1990, p. 8.

16. Merton P. Strommen and A. Irene Strommen, *Five Cries of Parents* (San Francisco: Harper and Row, 1985), p. 72.

17. Tim Kimmel, *Legacy of Love: A Plan for Parenting on Purpose* (Portland: Multnomah Press, 1989), p. 179.

18. Robert Laurent, *Keeping Your Teen in Touch with God* (Elgin, Illinois: David C. Cook Publishing Co, 1988), p. 111.

C H A P T E R   5

REKINDLING RELATIONSHIPS

Work at Getting Close to Your Teen

You may think you're the last person on earth your teenager wants to have a close relationship with, but don't be fooled. Teenagers are looking for adult interaction and affirmation in a desperate attempt to determine who they will become.

Ferndale High was my new frontier as a ninth-grader. I was excited to finally be in high school. But I'll never forget one particular day that occurred during my first quarter as a freshman. Everyone suited up for P.E. and marched out to line up against the wall of the old gymnasium. The new gym was for upperclassmen and varsity sports, so we got the old one—which had gaping holes in the ceiling tiles, and a scuffed and dented floor that was beyond repairing. The wooden walls were full of gashes and splinters, having been buffeted by sports events over the years.

We were picking teams for basketball. This was, to put it mildly, a downer for me. I just was not good at basketball. The selection process only accentuated that fact because I was always picked dead last, or close to last, to be on a team. My friends were not being consciously cruel, they just wanted good players—and I ranked way down on the list.

As it happened, I was standing with my back against the wall. One by one, others were picked ahead of me. Resigning myself to being picked last, I decided to sit down and wait it out. With my back still against the wall, I slid to the floor with a thud. Along the way down, a splinter of wood from the beat - up wall caught on my shorts, ripping them partially, and lodged itself in my behind.

Hitting the floor, I realized what had happened but did my best not to show any notice of it. Upon looking down, I was horrified to see a tiny trickle of blood running out from underneath my shorts. Roger Hansen noticed it, too. Immediately he pointed it out and began laughing. Every eye in the place turned toward me. Laughter broke out like a thousand symbols crashing over my head. My heart stopped. My glands swelled. My brain exploded. Someone yelled, "He's having a period!" Another round of ear-splitting laughter erupted. I wanted to die right on the spot.

Even the coach didn't come to my aid. He told the guys to shut up and ordered me to go clean up. I walked to the locker room holding the back of my shorts and feeling like a whipped dog. It took weeks to live down the episode.

As I write about it now, the whole incident makes me laugh out loud; but at the time, I prayed for death to end my embarrassment. What I would have given at that moment for a little reassurance, a shoulder to cry on, someone who was on my side. I felt stupid, isolated, and lonely—a mirror, in many ways, of how many teenagers feel much of the time.

The traumas of teenhood are many. More than ever, these young people need our support. Many walk the entire path of adolescence without feeling the deep and caring involvement of any adults—including their parents. They won't tell you they need you. They won't even act like it. But they do.

Adults today are incredibly busy people. They have planes to catch, people to meet, plans to make . . . and less time for young people. We can say what we want as we fly by; teenagers aren't dumb. They know that being busy is a choice and that if adults choose to spend their time on other things, they're choosing *not* to spend that time with them.

I have no idea who wrote it, but I found the following quip scribbled on a piece of paper deep in my desk: "This is the age of the half-read page and the quick bash and the mad dash. The bright night with the nerves tight. The plane hop with a brief stop. The lamp tan in a short span. The big shot in a good spot. And the brain strain and the heart pain and the cat naps till the spring snaps and the fun's done." Unfortunately, it's true.

JIMMY LOOKED AT ME as if I were his dad. "He's never around, and when he is he's sitting behind a newspaper and doesn't want to be bothered. It really gets to me. They're always complaining about how I'm never home anymore. What do they expect? When I *am* home, it's like I'm with a couple of people who aren't really there. And then they get all upset when I get in trouble or bring home a bad report card. What difference does it make? They never notice when I do anything right, so why try?"

"It feels pretty bad when you feel neglected, doesn't it?" I said after a minute of silence. Jimmy stared past me.

"Yeah," he answered, his voice trailing off. "I just don't care that much anymore."

AUTHOR URIE BRONFENBRENNER'S COMMENTS highlight a significant shift in the social conditions impacting teens of today as compared to the past, a past many parents of teens remember:

> Everybody in the neighborhood minded your business . . . . If you walked on the railroad trestle, the phone would ring at your house, and your parents would know what you had done before you got back home. People on the street would tell you to button your jacket, and ask why you were not in church last Sunday. Sometimes you liked it and sometimes you didn't—but at least people *cared* .[1]

Involvement has hit an all time low in American families and the panic of deprivation is settling in.

ROBERT CAUGHT ME NEAR the church entrance. "Hey, Daniel, is Jimmy doing any better in the youth group?" I wasn't sure how to respond. Nothing had really changed. Jimmy was scattered. He was distracting. He was obviously troubled. "Well," I stammered, "I think he's trying."

"We put him in a Christian school, you know. I think it's helping."

I knew we needed to talk. "Robert, how about doing breakfast with me? Maybe together we can help Jimmy."

"I'd love to," he responded. "I'll be out of town for five days beginning Tuesday, and next week is shot because of a convention down in San Diego. The following week, I'm heavy into meeting a sales deadline. Let me see . . . I think we could meet early one morning the week after that. Ooops! Forgot. I'll be in Pittsburgh that week to lead a training seminar for some of our novice sales force. Tell you what, I'll get back to you. Better yet, why don't you just meet with Elaine? She knows more about how to help Jimmy than I do anyway." He forced a half-laugh. "The kid just confuses me!" On the outside I smiled. Inside, I burned.

GETTING CLOSER TO OUR KIDS

Both parents work full-time in fifty-seven percent of all American families. For some that's a necessity for survival. For others it's a choice borne purely out of a drive to accumulate material things, or a need to prove our success. Since 1973, the average work week has gone from forty-one to forty-seven hours.[2] Consequently, between one fourth and one third of the children in America are coming home after school to empty houses.[3]

David, a 17-year-old senior, commented to me on this: "I admit I really like coming home to an empty house now. When I was younger I felt so lonely when I got home. Then I started sneaking my girlfriend into the house after school. That's when I first had sex. I was 14."

Not long ago, after a parents' seminar on teenagers at our church, I walked out into the parking lot with a nicely dressed man and his wife. Over the next twenty minutes or so, they told me how much they wished they had more time to spend with their kids, but that they were simply unable to find that time. In addition to both of them working full-time, he was an avid golfer, so there went his weekends. She was an avid shopper, so there went her weekends, along with the money she made at work. I mostly just listened, and soon they drove off in their gleaming new 4 X 4 truck.

I confess I couldn't help but wonder if they had ever considered *giving up* some of their possessions to give them time to work at another priority. I wondered if they realized Jimmy's life was staked on those things they clutched so tightly.

The prophetic words of Paul echo again: "They exchanged the truth of God for a lie, and worshiped and served created things rather than the Creator—who is forever praised" (Romans 1:25).

According to a recent study on "latchkey" kids, provided by the National Institute on Drug Use, young adolescents who are not given at least one hour of adult time each day are at greater risk for substance abuse, regardless of race, sex, academic performance, family income, or extracurricular activities. The study showed that the longer young adolescents are unsupervised, the greater their chances of abusing alcohol, tobacco, and marijuana.[5]

It has become apparent in recent years that all children desperately need to bond with the adult authorities in their lives in order to grow up emotionally well. Studies have indicated that this need is highest during the first couple of years of life, and then again in the early stages of adolescence.

Students in the Norman-Harris report were asked about the upsurge in teenage vandalism and what they felt might help stop it. Their number-one reply: "Parents need to pay more attention to their kids." Norman and Harris went on to speculate that a great deal of juvenile shoplifting is an unconscious attempt to signal a need for parental affection.[6] When the emotional needs for love and nurturing are not met, the result is an inner sense of sadness or depression, accompanied or followed by anger. Nothing has more clearly characterized this present generation of teens than *anger*.

So what does all this have to do with their faith? Absolutely everything, and that's why I bring it up. Many teens are so angry about their neglect that the efforts of adults to shape them spiritually are being met with sheer rebellion. Obviously, if faith is very important to a child's parents or others in authority over them, a powerful means of rebellion will be the rejection of the faith and values held by those adults they resent.

Remember Eli from the pages of Scripture past? Let's go back for a quick peek at a slice of history you'll easily identify with. Use your imagination to fill in the setting.

Eli slumped down in his seat before a table covered with rolled-up parchments. The stack was overwhelming. The afternoon had been a relentless whirlwind of complaints and arguments. Being a judge over the Israelites was no small task, and no matter how much time he applied to the job, the number of disgruntled people seemed to grow.

"I need some air," Eli grunted as he lifted his 200-pound frame from the seat. Opening the shutters, sounds of a conversation filtered up from the corridor below his window. Two women were talking, and Eli immediately realized the dialog was about him!

"Why in the world doesn't he do something about those sons of his? They call themselves priests but they're worse than the rest of us! I can't believe what they get away with. Not only are they stealing the temple offerings, but word has it they're carrying on affairs with the women who serve there!"

The other woman broke in. Eli felt flushed. "It's no secret anymore. I just can't figure out why Eli doesn't discipline them. Those kids ought to be brought before the elders and stoned to death, and Eli just carries on as if nothing were happening!"

"Well, something's got to happen soon," the other voice interjected. "If Eli doesn't stop what is going on, someone else is going to." Eli closed the window and stepped back.

Just last year a prophet from God had arrived at the temple. He had taken Eli into a back room and warned him. Those words continued to haunt his spirit. "Eli, thus saith the Lord your God, 'Why do you scorn my sacrifice and offering that I prescribed for my dwelling? Why do you honor your sons more than me by fattening yourselves on the choice parts of every offering made by my people Israel? Both of your sons are going to die on the same day, and I will raise up for myself a faithful priest who will do according to what is in my heart and mind.' Eli, listen to the words of God. You have not supervised your sons. You have busied yourself with the affairs of our people, to the exclusion of your own family. Eli, now they are going to die!"

Eli walked in the evening silence to his seat in the temple. Remorse weighed down each step, and tiredness burned in his eyes, now dim with old age. Sitting down, his thoughts drifted back over time. He had been a priest since he was young. He had served as judge over Israel for forty years. And . . . he had neglected his sons. Now, the deterioration was eating at the heart of the nation he loved. His sons were defaming God's decrees in the temple. They were prostituting the women. The Israelite army was being defeated by the Philistines, and Eli was an old man who had lost control.

Eli lifted his eyes to the ceiling of the temple and wondered. If only he had cared for his sons the way he cared for his work. If only he had instilled in them a heartfelt passion for God. If only he had balanced his life and given them his attention. But "if onlys" could not turn back time. History had been sealed (1 Samuel 2—4).

MONEY CAN'T BUY LOVE

Social scientists and psychologists today are bemoaning a disease that is plaguing this generation of teens in an unprecedented way. It's spreading and growing. Call it consumerism, name it materialism, write it off as inevitable, but the bottom line is that our children have become *greedy*.

I recently finished reading Henry Malcolm's book *Generation of Narcissus*. I heartily *don't* recommend it. I read it only because it mirrors so accurately the destructive self-absorption that characterizes our "brave new world." Malcolm explains that through unparalleled affluence, permissive child-rearing, progressive education, changing family relationships, and television, we have created a generation of young people who believe they live in a world that can be possessed and manipulated at will.

This "affluent child" views himself at the dead center of the universe, armed with the technological and intellectual tools he needs for manipulating his world. The questions "What is right?" and "What is wrong?" no longer need to be asked. Instead, the sole question has become, "Is this what you want?" Once you know what you want, then "just take it." This, then, is the basis for moral decision-making, according to Malcolm.[7]

One girl explained, "I don't understand why adults talk about money all the time, dream about all the junk they want, buy more and more stuff, and then scold us when we want something. All my dad ever talks about is wanting a sailboat. If I even say I want another pair of shoes, he goes into this tirade about how ungrateful I am."

While there are obviously many factors contributing to this excess, one of the most significant is that we as a culture have been trained to think material consumption has something to do with our capacity for joy. In other words, through slick advertising and social modeling, we're conditioned to believe that the more we have, the happier we feel. The teens of this decade are bombarded with this errant philosophy. Madonna speaks for millions when she says, "I'm a material girl." But at the same time, kids sense the hollowness of it all.

The problem is compounded when well-meaning adults depend heavily on material goods to communicate care for young people. Spending is easier than interacting, and so we too perpetrate the lie. More than ever, we have attempted to fatten this generation on goods, hoping they'll be happy because of it. Consequently, the relational anorexia just keeps eating away at our teens.

Ralph and Pat Van Peursem have four children, all of whom have grown into adulthood possessing a real love for God and the practice of serving others. The Van Peursems talked about their kids and material things:

> Though they rarely had the 'right clothes' or a car or money or whatever, they were aware many were less fortunate. We sometimes did and sometimes didn't provide "that label" or certain things perceived as bringing acceptance. It was hard on them, and on us, to see Christian kids include or reject other Christian kids on such superficial grounds. It taught them to look beyond the surface in their relationships.

THEY NEED SOMEONE TO LEAN ON

Like a dizzying "Mr. Toad's Wild Ride" at Disneyland, teenagers are breaking into adulthood. The process involves some drastic changes and developmental tasks. They are adjusting to: the physical changes of puberty; a flood of impulses brought on by genital maturity; a new-found independence from parents or other adult caretakers; the beginning of effective social and working relationships with both those of the same sex and those of the opposite sex; preparation for a vocation; the establishment of beliefs and behavioral patterns; and the development of a personal sense of identity.

I RECEIVED AN ANONYMOUS note. Three weeks later, Karen confessed she had written it. "I kept thinking about how my friends talk about me behind my back. I tried to talk to them but they were always too busy. I felt like, no matter what I did, I couldn't please my mom and dad. Then one night everyone was gone. I was alone and I felt so lonely. I didn't even know what I was doing. I just started tearing through my brother's bathroom looking for his razor blades. All I thought about was how they'd feel if I died. I wanted them to realize I wasn't just making things up when I told them how terrible my life was.

"I took the razor into my room and cut my wrist—not very deep. I sat there on the bed staring at the little bit of blood that was coming out. I wasn't even crying. I was just so angry that no one cared about me. Finally I realized this was stupid and I put a bandage on my wrist. I still think about suicide all the time. Why doesn't anyone take me seriously?"

TEENAGERS ARE SLOWLY PIECING life together. They're desperately trying to focus on this new world of theirs. They're catching their balance. When parents or other significant adults aren't close by for support, that process of gaining stability becomes a nightmare. To ask for our assistance would be a gross betrayal, so they feel, of the independence that is attempting to emerge from within. Yet, not having our support leaves them without a source of wisdom and encouragement to draw on. It puts them in a precarious position — like sitting ducks that are ready for something else, or someone else, to grab them. The depression they feel is real, and in some cases it can be deadly.

EXAMINE THEIR RELATIONAL NEEDS

One of the most attractive qualities in teenagers is their sheer love of *relating*. Most of them thrive on it. They love to talk on the phone and laugh and wrestle and tell stories and hear stories and debate issues and share feelings and care for hurting people and stay up late having heart-to-heart discussions. Their capacity for relating on a personal level seems endless.

Not only that, but one of the fundamental tasks they face as adolescents is to explore all angles of human relationships. Expressing their opinion, giving up their time for someone else, resolving conflicts, being honest, expressing anger, listening effectively, showing affection, and other relational traits, are in the furnace of refinement. Adult interaction at this point in their lives provides a much-needed link with an image of who they can and will become. Adults who are close provide a test market for the relational skills teens are experimenting with.

Larry, Steve, and Dave Ross are all active in Christian service. Larry is a press agent for Billy Graham, Steve and his family are missionaries in Peru, and Dave works part-time as a writer and director of church theatrical productions. I asked their parents, Art and Ruth Ross, what they would share with other parents from their own experiences. Art said:

> Respect and esteem your teenager! Their tastes in music and dress are often not the same as ours. Not all of it is rebellion. Learn to roll with some of the passing fads and make an effort to listen to their lyrics and cries to be heard. Enter into their world and schedule and make them feel that their interests are important to you. Spend as much time with them as possible without grudging. When I think of the number of times I put them off for my own interests and responsibilities, I wish I had the years back to do it over again. In spite of human failure, God touched each boy in a special way.

If Ruth could have the years back again, she would make time to really listen to her teenagers more. In her busy schedule, she would often listen with one ear while she was concentrating on something else (although the boys have a higher estimate of her interest span than she does). She would also try to be a better role model in patience and acceptance of unexpected interruptions. Teenagers need our interest in their world and friends. They deserve receiving our undivided attention when they are confiding to us their hurts and joys.

Teenagers want and need to feel our sincere joy in being with them. They want to feel as though they're viewed like adults in some ways, that they are close to you like a friend, that they leave you feeling good when they're gone. It's our job to communicate that we really do take pleasure in them in countless ways. It needs to be stated and affirmed over and over again.

GET CLOSE TO HELP THEM SEE CHRIST

More than any other source, adults who love God and are living out their faith in Christ provide impetus for teens to do the same. Let's imagine two family scenarios. Both sets of parents are Christians and value biblical ethics.

In the first family, both parents work full-time. Mom and Dad are shining examples of Christian character. They maintain strict guidelines for behavior in their children, and homework must be completed before the television gets turned on. Mom is a school teacher and has PTA or some other school function at least one night a week. Dad is a businessman who is out of town one to two weeks a month.

Mom attends a fellowship and support group for women on Tuesday evenings, and when Dad is in town the two of them go to a Wednesday evening Bible study at church. Dad has Toastmasters on Thursdays. The kids are busy with band and baseball practice and going out with friends in the evenings and on the weekends, but they are expected to spend at least ten minutes each day having a "quiet time" with the Lord. On Saturdays, Dad normally goes golfing (when he's in town), and Sundays after church are reserved for naps. After all, everyone is pretty tired. Sunday evening affords another church service, and the week begins again.

Family number two doesn't look quite as polished. Mom works part-time and Dad's construction business has ups and downs, so finances are never very constant. Dad is off to the construction site early, but Mom sits at the breakfast table for about half an hour and chats with the kids as they fly through the routine of downing their cereal and toast. When the kids get home, Dad usually isn't far behind. Dad has tried to quit smoking a number of times but his breath is bad, and it's obvious he's still addicted.

Early evenings find Dad helping the kids with their homework or shooting hoops in the driveway. Mom gets home by 6:00, and dinner becomes a forum for discussion of the day's problems and joys. Dad opens the Bible and fumbles through a passage. He applies it to life as best he can, but the devotion usually gets off on a tangent that lasts for a half-hour or more, with more than one person talking at once. Everyone attends a Bible study on Wednesday nights, and the kids have the usual string of other activities, but for the most part, all or part of the family is home together many evenings. On Sunday the family goes to church and then usually rides bikes or takes a picnic to the beach or just "hangs out" at home.

Now, while neither family is perfect, which family would you lay your money on? Whose kids are going to see Christ? I'd pick family number two, although not everyone would agree.

Teenagers aren't looking for perfection in adults half as much as they're looking for honesty. They're looking for someone with flesh on, someone who will enter into the day-to-day struggle along with them. Adults who can freely admit that they, too, are in process, that they, too, sin and receive God's forgiveness, are setting the stage for those same healthy attitudes in the young people who watch them.

The disciples followed Christ and His teaching for one reason: He loved them. He didn't cram the truth down their throats or lay on heavy guilt trips or expect them to catch it from the ancient writings themselves. He lived with them and he loved them. The result? They *believed* Him. When it comes to adopting values, the power of love and admiration cannot be overstated.

RANDY MET ME AT Taco Bell and plopped his new Bible down on the top of my desk. "Got it for my birthday," he informed me.

I grabbed the Bible and began leafing through it. "You're amazing," I said. "You've already got a bunch of verses highlighted!"

"Nope," Randy objected. "My dad did it. He went through and highlighted a whole bunch of verses before he gave it to me. He said they were the ones that changed *his* life . . . He said they would change mine, too. He said I should try to memorize some of them. I couldn't believe he took the time to do that. In fact, look . . . "

Randy went on a random shopping-spree type search for various marked passages, reading them aloud to me once he found them. I sat there staring at a real, normal teenager, surrounded by a swarm of fast-food patrons, who was getting excited about God's Truth. *Somewhere out there,* I thought to myself, *is a dad who really cares about his kid.* Cared enough to add a personal touch to his exhortations about Truth. Because of that, the Truth was hitting home. It was sinking in. It was changing a life.

GETTING CLOSE THROUGH OUR PRAYERS

My parents never followed me around, or (to my knowledge) ever snooped through my stuff or called others to check up on me. What they *did* do was hold a daily prayer vigil in my honor. They prayed about my choices and friends and dates and driving habits. The knowledge of their prayers haunted me when temptations arose, and comforted me when the blows of adolescence hit hard. Their prayers were like a guardian angel that followed me day and night. Nothing could have given me a greater sense of their twenty-four-hour love and concern than to know their prayers were continuously ascending.

The frustrating angle on prayer is that it often doesn't show immediate results. There are days when it does, but more days when it doesn't seem to, and those are the days when hope grows thin and prayer seems pointless. Prayer generally shows its power down the pike. It is then that we can look back and see the paths that were paved, the people that changed, the strongholds that were broken. We see how true it is that God listens and responds. We see in the long haul what is hidden in the short run.

I mentioned the Van Peursems earlier. At one point they simply didn't know what else to do but pray.

> Our son Ron really enjoyed secular rock music, and some of the lyrics were horrible. We told him how we felt, and pointed out how it was detrimental to him, as well as to us as a family. We showed him how it

would affect his relationship with the Lord. Although we couldn't control what he did when we weren't around, we put restrictions on his playing it at home. We prayed for his protection and awareness of the effect it had on him. Then, four years later, he called from Humbolt State University to say he had destroyed the albums. He had finally become aware of how it was affecting him. There were so many situations like that, where God answered our prayers.

How important is your prayer time to you? Your prayer time may be the most important thing in the world to your teen.

BREAKING DOWN THE BARRIERS

I was dreaming about a loud humming noise when I regained enough consciousness to lean over and hit the travel alarm. Rolling off the upper bunk, my feet hit the frozen stone floor with a thud. It was an ungodly 5:00 A.M., but that's when I was supposed to wake him. "Dad," I whispered in the dark. "Dad, get up." He moaned and rolled over to see his twenty-three-year-old son standing there shivering in his underwear. "It's five o'clock; we've gotta go."

Three weeks earlier we'd met at Ben Gurion Airport in Tel Aviv. My father was living overseas, and I was enrolled in seminary. Since I was going to be studying in Israel these weeks, Dad had decided to join me and tour the country with me. There would be no showers this morning. The "fortress" we were housed in, just outside the old wall of Jerusalem, didn't have hot water until about seven A.M. And then only if you were sly enough to get in before it was all gone. No race this morning.

Bundled in sweats and an overcoat, I tiptoed out of the dorm room and through a dark hallway which led outside. It was raining. And freezing! A ten-minute walk would put us at the taxi stop where Dad was to catch his ride to the airport. I stood under the awning, waiting for my father to finish packing his last few things and join me. Misty rain looked like drops of gold, illumined as it was by the amber street light. And there beyond, not more than fifty yards away, was the massive wall of Jerusalem. Lit by flood lights, it stood magnificent against the black night.

A week earlier my father and I had taken a morning walk along the wall. We followed the sidewalk which extends along the western side of the city, just outside of the wall, running from the southern tip where we were staying to the northern tip. There, an overweight Jewish baker owned a tiny shop that featured the best bagels east of Manhattan.

As we walked that morning, I launched into a discussion with my father about the things that had disappointed me about his parenting. While some of those things were true, my delivery was miserable. The keynote address focused on his lack of involvement with me growing up.

Dad and I had never had a lot of "deep" conversations. I was raised knowing his love, but not a lot of his mind. He was a quiet guy, with the patience and humility of Jesus. And he was an excellent father, but not one that exuded much emotion. For some reason I had one grunt of adolescence left down inside, and I needed to unload it that morning.

I told him how I wished he'd spent more time with me, how it bugged me that he communicated so little, and without a smattering of passion, and how shallow our relationship seemed to me. And he just took it. That's how he is. He said something about how communicating his feelings had always been hard but that he loved me, and he hoped I knew that. We stared at the wall for a while. Then we walked on.

I've often thought about the walls that separate our lives from the lives of those we love the most. Walls are constructed a stone at a time—by other interests, weeks away on business, our inability to express thoughts in words, and by our own inhibitions. Walls are thin when kids are young. But as they grow, schedules complicate and activities differ, straining communication. And walls thicken.

But it's never too late to start chiseling. Like a Berlin Wall being smashed away bit by bit and carried off, we too can dismantle the barriers that isolate us from each other. It requires an honest evaluation of where our time is going and how our love is getting across. And we need to ask God for His help. We can trust Him to put the chisel in our hand.

NOTES:

1. Urie Bronfenbrenner, *Two Worlds of Childhood: U.S. and U.S.S.R.* (New York: Russel Sage Foundation, 1970), p. 96.

2. Nancy Gibbs, "How America Has Run Out of Time," *Time*, 24 April 1989, pp. 58-60.

3. Charles Swindoll, *Growing Wise in Family Life* (Portland: Multnomah, 1988), p. 20.

4. "Latchkey Kids at Risk with Drugs," *Christian Parenting Today*, January/February 1990, p. 66.

5. Jane Norman and Myron Harris, *The Private Life of the American Teenager* (New York: Rawson, Wade Publishers, Inc., 1981), pp. 255-258.

6. Henry Malcolm, *Generation of Narcissus* (Boston: Little Brown and Company, 1971), p. 153.

DOING IS BELIEVING

Offer Experiences that Demand Choices

G*iving lip service to Christianity only breeds lethargy and boredom. Conversely, a genuine love for God that results in a radical life of faith and action is a most intense and dynamic way to live. Teenagers are at a point where they need to experience this thrill for themselves!*

The climb seemed more treacherous than ever. Abraham was no stranger to this type of climbing. He was always climbing this mountain or that hill in order to build an altar to God. He was accustomed to making animal sacrifices for repentance or for thanksgiving. But today everything was different. Every step took effort.

His faith had been tried when God called Abraham to leave his home and friends in the land of Ur to establish a new nation in Canaan. His faith had waned over the years as he waited for the fulfillment of God's promise of a son, who finally was born — much to everyone's surprise. But now, this was too much!

A jagged rock cut into the sole of his shoe. Abraham reached for Isaac's shoulder to keep from losing his balance. He was old now. He was tired. And he had been sure Isaac had been born to fulfill God's promise that He would establish a nation through Abraham's descendants. But this?

Just the day before, God had spoken to Abraham directly; there was no doubt about it. God had said, "Abraham, take your son, your only son, Isaac, whom you love, and go to the region of Moriah. Sacrifice him there as a burnt offering on one of the mountains I will tell you about."

Every step became heavier. The two of them were nearing the top. Abraham's mind was racing. "Why is God doing this? He knows my faith is strong. Why would he ask me to do this horrible thing to my son? "Dad?" Isaac's young voice broke the silence. "We have the fire and the wood, but where is the lamb for the burnt offering?" Abraham couldn't take it any longer. His eyes filled with tears. Turning away to hide his face, Abraham quietly replied in strained tones, "God will provide it, Isaac. God will provide."

A hot breeze whistled in the silence of the mountain's peak. Abraham built an altar out of stones, and Isaac helped him carefully arrange the twigs and pieces of wood for the fire. "Please, son, don't ask any questions. Don't say a word." Abraham took some rope from inside his garment and began to tie up Isaac's hands and feet. Isaac's heart filled with panic, but he trusted his father and remained silent. Abraham lifted the boy onto the altar and set him, ever so gently, onto the wood. With trembling hands, he reached into his satchel and fumbled for the knife.

Isaac was in shock. Abraham closed his eyes and, with fear nearly paralyzing every muscle in his body, he slowly raised the knife over Isaac's throat. Instantly a thunderous voice boomed, "ABRAHAM!" The knife fell to the ground. Abraham dropped to his knees, shaking, with his face turned skyward. "Do not lay a hand on the boy," he heard the voice speak with urgency. "Do not do anything to him. Now I know that you fear God, because you have not withheld from me your son, your only son." The voice was gone. Abraham sat motionless.

A rustling nearby caught his attention. There in a thicket of bushes not more than a few yards away, he saw a ram entangled in some vines. Abraham jumped to his feet and unbound Isaac. The two of them tied the ram and lifted it onto the altar for the sacrifice.

Again the voice from heaven filled the air: "I swear by myself, that because you have done this and have not withheld your son, your only son, I will surely bless you and make your descendants as numerous as the stars in the sky and as the sand on the seashore. Your descendants will take possession of the cities of their enemies, and through your offspring all nations on earth will be blessed, because you have obeyed me" (Genesis 22).

Abraham wasn't a superman. He was just very committed. He was a simple man who was convinced that true belief was authenticated by action. He lived what he believed. He acted on God's word. He made the sacrifice.

Teenagers don't do that naturally. None of us do. But we can learn to do it, one action at a time.

INFUSING CHOICE-MAKING WITH VALUES

Adolescents generally have a much harder time refining moral behavior than they do generating an openness to spiritual things. We often judge them as having little spiritual capacity just because their behavioral choices are at times so poor. Turning faith into behavioral patterns is slow, grueling work. Just because they may appear to an outsider to be "footloose and fancy free," with little thought for moral restraint, don't be fooled. On the inside, most teenagers are grappling with the meaning of it all.

Karen shared this observation with me: "My parents must think I agree with everything I do. I don't. A lot of times I do things that I know are wrong. But when they find out what I've done, they lecture me about how wrong it was. I already know that."

Despite the apparent slowness of processing belief into behavior, teenagers actually do form actions out of the mortar of their beliefs. Search Institute, operating out of Minneapolis, Minnesota, conducted an extensive "Adolescent-Parent Survey," gaining insight from 8,165 randomly selected young adolescents and 10,467 of their parents. Search found that as acceptance of traditional beliefs goes up, antisocial behaviors, drug and alcohol use, norm violations, and promiscuity, go down.

The Search team also found that those teens who reported having a "religious faith that was central and important" were more inclined toward helping, serving, and having a proper sense of self-esteem.[1]

More than a hundred studies are documented which show a significant correlation between beliefs and moral restraint. Conversely, loss of moral beliefs can be shown to be associated with a rise in immoral, illegal, and self-destructive behaviors.[2]

Teenagers need to see clearly how their beliefs can and should shape their behavior. When quizzed about what they believe or value, most would score high. Then the score drops when it comes to behavior. Many teens don't even see the connection. They need to be *taught* the connection. For instance, let's look at some God-given values and consider how they might possibly translate into behaviors. Notice that God's values are eternal and never-changing, while our responses to those, the actions we take, may vary depending on our circumstances. There are countless proper actions that can be taken based on our beliefs. This is where wisdom and discernment must be developed with practice.

MY BELIEFS — MY BEHAVIOR

I value other's property. *I won't shoplift.*

I value beauty and order. *I won't destroy public property.*

I value the elderly. *I will visit those in rest homes.*

I value sexual purity. *I won't compromise sexually.*

I value clear judgment. *I won't abuse drugs.*

I value all people. *I won't discriminate.*

I value kindness. *I won't gossip about others.*

I value compassion. *I will take action to stop hunger.*

I value honesty. *I will tell the truth.*

I value God's creation. *I will protect it.*

I value my body as God's temple. *I won't abuse alcohol.*

I value wisdom. *I will try hard in school.*

It wasn't long ago that one of the girls in my group came to me with a most common complaint: everyone else was "cliquish," everyone but her, of course. She couldn't understand why they weren't more loving. As she talked, this whole idea of people not being loving enough kept coming to the forefront so finally I asked, "Sabrena, be 100 percent honest with me for a moment, OK?" She agreed.

"Have you ever gossiped about anyone in our group?"

"Yes," she admitted somewhat defiantly.

"More than once?"

"Yeah."

Then I carefully exhorted her: "Sabrena, every one of us is just like you. We all want to feel close to our friends. So to try and impress them and hold on to them, we shut others out, in a lot of different ways. In my opinion, the most deadly and unloving way is to gossip about them; yet, we've all done it. Have you ever thought about the fact that love would never gossip about another person? To love means to speak in a supportive way of others, no matter what, even when they fail us. Love in a group of people like our youth group will only begin when people like you become loving."

"I guess I never thought about it that way before," Sabrena answered. By the end of our conversation we had examined the relationship between the value of loving others and not gossiping about them. The connection, for Sabrena, was a completely novel idea.

ACTION—THE LITMUS TEST OF FAITH

We may say the deal looks good, but would we put our money on it? We may say we believe our son is a good driver, but how do we react when we're in the car, and he's behind the wheel? We may say we love people, but do our sacrifices for them match our claims? Nothing convinces like action. When we're mobilized to live what we say we believe, our own convictions are strengthened and our witness to others at last has substance.

Larry and Terry Keelin stressed this in their comments on having raised two teenagers who love God:

> We talked about values, but, more importantly, we as parents tried to live out what we said. We didn't set a lot of rules, but let them know that there are consequences to all of our choices. We never expected them to do what we wouldn't do ourselves. You've got to be real with your children, letting them know that you are not perfect, but that we can do all things through Christ.

Teens are observing us round the clock. They're watching how we spend our money, our time, and our energy. They're watching how we strengthen, defend, and articulate our faith. They're seeing how we make decisions and judgments. They're noticing how we admit to failures and what we do in a crisis. They're taking it all in and they're deciding if faith is something that works.

Just as a football game can't be won in the huddle, Christianity also must be proven on the "playing field," in the grisly fight of everyday life. If you ask teenagers what they believe to be true, they will most often reflect on what they have seen and experienced, as opposed to what they've been told is true.

In June of 1973, my parents gathered some of their savings and we headed to the country of Ghana, on the West coast of Africa, to work there for a summer. Being teachers by profession, my folks took positions in a small Bible college established to train local people in the Christian faith. Even though I was of junior high age at the time, Mom and Dad put me to work at the mission headquarters, helping with mailings and involving myself in the mission's ministry of literature distribution. I felt needed, and I experienced what it meant to make sacrifices because of what we valued.

During our three months there, we traveled to various parts of the country, giving away portions of the Bible printed in the native dialects, visiting and encouraging pastors who ministered in the jungle, or the "bush" as they called it, giving supplies to those who were destitute, and sharing our faith whenever we had the opportunity. It changed my life forever. Why? Because we as a family put our faith on the line. We put works behind our words, and met the challenge of acting out our faith head on.

Mike Yacconelli and Jim Burns wrote about the role service plays in the development of faith:

> There is a practical way to get the truth into kids' lives — service. The more kids are given the opportunity to serve others, the more real their faith becomes. The more kids can focus on others rather than on themselves, the more they will begin to understand the needs and hurts of others. The more kids can minister to those who suffer, the more they understand the ministry of the One who suffered for us all. If we want high school students to have a personal faith that functions in the real world, then we need to teach them to serve.[3]

GOING TO BAT AGAINST APATHY

In a day and age when opportunities abound, most teens are feeling underchallenged and apathetic. When I say underchallenged, I'm not referring to their schedules. They are busier than ever. They've got tons of homework, a job at the mall, a car to fix, friends to meet, and a full schedule of athletics, not to mention enough nonstop amusements to keep them occupied constantly.

Karen couldn't have looked more bored. "So what do you want to do with your life?" I asked, posing a fairly broad inquiry in the hope she would grab the opportunity to express herself. "Nothing," came the reply. I was somewhat taken back. "What do you mean by 'nothing'?" I asked. "Isn't there *something* you'd like to do?"

"I guess just get married."

"What about God? Do you ever feel like you could make a difference in this world? You know, help people or pour your life into something that will outlast it?"

"I've never thought about it," she responded.

"What *do* you think about?" I asked.

Karen paused for a moment, then said, "I guess my friends and clothes and stuff. I worry about what I'm going to do in the future but I don't know what to do about it."

I continued, "What do you see in yourself that you're good at? What skills or interests do you have that you could use to make a difference in other people's lives?"

"I don't know," Karen shot back, sounding a little annoyed. "I've never done anything that made any difference to anyone."

Karen's plight isn't uncommon among teens. She and many like her have never tasted of usefulness. They've never been given a vision for greatness by becoming a servant to others. It's a wild concept that they've never considered. It's a fulfillment they know nothing about.

Most teens need some hands-on experiences in order to process the possibility that there is something more worthwhile and profound in life than just the self-absorbing "stuff" of American culture. More than ever, teenagers in America are feeling bored and empty. How can that be when they have more wealth, technology and options for pleasure than ever before in the history of the world? They're apathetic because all this "excitement" isn't producing what it promised.

Bellingham, Washington is not the most exciting place in the world in which to grow up. Most travel agencies don't list it as a "fabulous vacation destination." About the biggest event that ever came to town, at least in the eyes of a young kid, was the carnival that rolled in every spring. For one week the lights would flash, the motors would roar, the food would flow, and the rides would spin. It was dizzying and wonderful to someone my age.

On one particular night, I rode on the Rock-O-Plane with my friends. Soon after, I realized that somehow I had lost all the change in my pockets. Only a moment of thought brought about the realization that the ride I had just enjoyed probably had shaken the money right out of my pants.

My friends and I hurried back to the ride and stood there, watching. As we suspected, it wasn't long before we heard the tinkling of someone's change falling through the bars to the pavement below. It fell at the feet of the ride operator. It now belonged to him. Sadly, I remember walking away realizing there was no way in the world I was ever going to get my money back.

Life in America is dizzying, too. Step right up! Look at the lights! Here's a new video game. Nonstop action. Get a hot new car. Catch it on the big screen. Now you can have it all. Buy this, it'll make you feel like a million. This is the life. Here's to good times! Bottoms up! Hey kid, wanna try a new "high"? Need some lovin'? No problem, step inside for a peek. Eat some more. Live it up. You only go around once! Got a headache?— we've got a pill! Around and around it goes and where it stops . . . only hell knows.

When there is a rare lull in the action or when the lights go out for the night—and suddenly there's a flash of sanity— teenagers realize it's all a rip-off. It leaves them empty and stripped. What value they came in with is gone when they leave. Their longings for "life abundant" never materialize, and they wander past all the thrill hawkers feeling deeply shaken.

That's where the magic of sacrificial service comes in. It releases us from the boredom of self-preoccupation. It allows us to feel what we long to feel but haven't felt in a long time. In a strange way, personal identity is restored when we're given the chance to go beyond our selfish lusts. Like a life-filled breeze running over us, sacrificial love bestowed freely on others has a way of blowing away all the superficial trappings of our affluence and allows us to glimpse a supernatural quality in ourselves and those whom we serve.

PRAXIS MAKES PERFECT

"Praxis" is the name social "experts" have given to the process of developing convictions through a grid of experiences. As the theory goes, an individual will construct a view on life, or, what they consider truth to be, through interpretation of personal struggle. Those who believe in praxis would contend that what a person *does* determines what he will *believe.* To put it another way: Action will determine personal convictions.[4]

Now, we could go further, digging through the implications and ramifications of this theory; but for our purposes that isn't necessary. What is important is to realize that teenagers arrive at what they believe to be true through the use of praxis without even knowing that they're doing it. Any amount of time spent with young people will reveal that much of their religious conviction is indeed based on what they have experienced.

I COULDN'T BELIEVE IT, but Karen agreed to go on a summer mission to the ghettos of Mexico City. In fact, she seemed excited for the first time in a long time. She got signed up. She raised support. She finished her junior year and took off one week later. Karen wasn't exactly what you'd call "most likely to succeed," but they took her anyway.

From day one, Karen was given jobs—cooking and washing dishes, unpacking luggage, and setting up her tent in the rain in under five minutes. She was forced to work with others just to survive. On top of that, she had a regular schedule of Scripture memory, and they taught her how to share her faith with others. She was made a part of a ministry team that performed skits and sang to people about the Truth of God. She interacted with new people, new cultures, and new awareness. In short, she was mobilized into action with a "sink or swim" approach.

Slowly Karen began to see that loving God made a difference to those around her. She felt the power of their love. She felt needed and important and believed in. She was being jump-started into owning convictions about what was true.

Over those two months, stirrings of new life were spotted by those around her. Karen was changing.

Teenagers must be exposed to situations and environments that demand conviction and action from them. Until the pressure of expectation is on, there is little motivation to perform morally or responsibly. Practical life situations have a way of ironing ethics into the fabric of our personalities.

While not every kid responds immediately (in fact, most *don't),* opportunities for action, coupled with time, will result in a foundation for internalizing what must be true. Despite what you or I say, or even model, until they *experience* Truth, that Truth will most often be suspect or rejected altogether.

FEELING IS BELIEVING

In his incredible book, *The Power of the Powerless,* author Christopher de Vinck shares with tremendous insight what life was like growing up beside a severely handicapped brother. Through caring for his brother Oliver, he learned about love, shared pain, and self-sacrifice. He writes:

> Oliver grew to the size of a ten-year-old. He had a big chest, a large head. His hands and feet were those of a five-year-old. We'd wrap a box of baby cereal for him at Christmas and place it under the tree. We'd pat his head with a damp cloth in the middle of a July heat wave. His baptismal certificate hung on the wall above his head. A bishop came to the house and confirmed him.

> Oliver still remains the most hopeless human being I ever met and the weakest human being I ever met, and yet he was one of the most powerful human beings I ever met.

> As a teacher, I spend many hours preparing my lessons, hoping that I can influence my students in small, significant ways. Thousands of books are printed each year with the hope that the authors can

move people to action. We all labor at the task of raising our children, teaching them values, hoping something "gets through" to them after all our efforts.

Oliver could do absolutely nothing except breathe, sleep, eat and yet he was responsible for action, love, courage, insight. For me, to have been brought up in a house where a tragedy was turned into a joy, explains to a great degree why I am the type of husband, father, writer and teacher I have become.[5]

Teenagers long for challenges like that. They want to feel real love for others. They really want to give of themselves. They really want to make a difference in the world. But often their potentials are not recognized and their spirits are left simply to conform to the self-gratifying drone of the world they live in.

TAKIN' IT TO THE STREETS

While parents and adults can model, describe, explain, discuss, and exhort, they cannot internalize for a teen. When all is said and done, every teenager must individually come to grips with the reality of personal faith. The best way to confront them with that is to submerge them in experiences that exact decision from them. They must be pinned against the wall a little, forced to make some tough choices, feel the thrill of good choices versus the agony of poor ones. That involves risk: risk of danger, of not performing well, of embarrassing our trainers.

When challenged, my experience has been that teens do an even better job of responding to Christ's admonitions toward service and sacrifice than adults do. Verses like these can trigger real responses in young people:

"If anyone would come after me, let him deny himself, and take up his cross daily, and follow me" (Luke 9:23).

"Anyone who does not give up everything he has cannot be my disciple" (Luke 14:33).

"Whatever man loses his life for my sake will find it" (Matthew 10:39).

"Go into all the world and preach the good news to all creation" (Mark 16:15).

We must not only give them the admonition to go and serve, but need to put ourselves on the line to let them.

Each year the Mission Hills Student Gathering takes thirty junior high kids into the center of the worst part of Los Angeles. We park our vans and walk the dirty streets awhile, before ending up at one of the downtown "rescue mission" ministries. After a quick tour of the facility, the students are put to work washing tables, sorting clothes, serving meals, and interacting with the people who have come for help. We can talk and talk and talk about the importance of helping the poor. But until we put ourselves in gear, it's little more than . . . talk.

Adolescent character transformation comes primarily through life experiences that flesh out what kids have heard over and over. While there is nothing wrong with the saying and the hearing, these functions will never translate into positive action and service for teens until they are shown how to serve as a natural course of living. What's exciting is that once students discover their ability to make a positive impact on others, it's like a whole new dimension of their character is released. Sound overly dramatic? I would have thought so too, if it hadn't happened to me. Every year I watch it take place in the lives of teenagers.

A good example of this is allowing a teenager to serve the Lord in a missions program. While one of the greatest opportunities before Christian parents today is the chance to send their young people overseas for a summer missions project, I've seen parents recoil in fear and refuse to let their kids go. Naturally, it's a tough step of faith to take. But it is the kind of practical step required in order to allow our teens to taste the Truth.

Every couple of years I take a group of high school students to Europe for a month-long backpack trip. The students work for a year to raise the money they need to go. Finally, after a lot of effort they pull it off, and we set out on our adventure. During the following four weeks we visit numerous missionary operations, interact with the local people, learn some of the history of each of the countries we visit, develop an appreciation for art and culture, and serve each other as brothers and sisters in ways we never do at home. We set a goal of reading through most of the New Testament during the month, and most of the students make it. We share our faith on trains and with international students in youth hostels.

Every day we meet together to elaborate on what we're seeing, learning, and experiencing. We level with each other about things that have irritated us. We confess our failures in an atmosphere of forgiveness and acceptance. We exact from one another a level of maturity most have never experienced. The impact of all this is astounding. Obviously the trip is only one cog in a larger wheel of experience, but it is an important one; and nearly all the students who have made this trip are now active in ministry to others. I think all of them would point to that month as a turning point in their Christian faith. We take what we say we believe and then learn to live it.

Not all learning experiences need to be so organized or grandiose. Some of our best "faith-in-action" experiences happen during the course of everyday life. For instance, how do you respond when:

- **You see someone stranded by the side of the road struggling to change a tire? What values would you be teaching if you stopped to help?**

- **You're asked to give up watching a really important football game to set up chairs for a church function? What are you saying by your attitudes and actions?**

- **You hear of a walk-a-thon to raise money in support of the pro-life movement? What difference** would your "pro-life" words make if you considered a walk-a-thon too much of an inconvenience?

- Your son tells you about a poor family that barely has enough to eat, while you're planning a big Thanksgiving feast? What if you and your son were to take that family a portion of each of the dishes you made and serve them a Thanksgiving meal?

- You hear of an opportunity to sponsor a needy child overseas for $21 a month? Imagine if each family member or kid in your small group pitched in $5 a month from their allowance or earnings and together you sponsored a child.

- You pass a rest home every day on the way to and from your house. What if one Saturday you all baked cookies and placed them on paper plates, with Scripture verses written on those plates, and took them to those lonely people?

My list barely scratches the surface. You and your teenager could come up with a much better one. The key is to have the teens themselves help design the "acts of faith." Service will probably be thwarted by apathy unless they are inspired to choose and organize what goes on. Give everyone control of one idea, and facilitate their efforts at directing it.

FOR OVER SIX MONTHS Gary had been looking for a job. I called to find out how it was going and was surprised by what I discovered.

"I'm working at a home for old people," Gary related. He sounded more alive than ever. "Yeah, there are seven old people that live in the place, and there are two nurses there, too. It's like a big family. It's cool." I was stunned.

"You like working there?" I responded, trying to mask my disbelief. "Yeah, they think of me like I'm their grandson." He laughed. "I bring my friends over to meet them and they think it's funny that I'm working here. They freak out when I show 'em my tattoos. I take care of them—you know. I help them get around and bring them their food. There is this one old guy I have to feed. He can't even feed himself. Sometimes we go on field trips to the zoo or to the mall. They really dig on it."

I was no less than astonished. After we hung up, I sat there completely still for a moment, trying to process what I'd just heard. That was months ago now, and Gary is still there. He's doing well. And I continue to be amazed. The fact is, Gary finally found a safe place. He found, surprisingly, a group of powerless people that don't threaten him. He's finding that he can make a difference in people's lives. He's even taking a couple of classes at our local community college, and sticking with it—a small step in the right direction for the first time in years.

"There is this one lady who always wants me to read her Bible to her. I look up stuff for her and read it to her because her eyes are really bad," Gary told me a few weeks back.

Only God knows what the days ahead will hold for Gary. But for now, his heart is softening. His awareness of God is beginning to dawn. He's experiencing the reality of a life that counts, and it feels right.

Nothing will inspire a motivation toward love and goodness like the smell of personal sweat and the feel of hands calloused by service to others who cannot repay. It's a formula that produces the very qualities that make for a genuinely Christian life. It's up to us to provide an arena in which this miracle can take place.

NOTES:

1. Merton P. Strommen and A. Irene Strommen, *Five Cries of Parents* (San Francisco: Harper and Row, 1985), p. 138.

2. Ibid., p. 138.

3. Mike Yaconelli and Jim Burns, *High School Ministry* (Grand Rapids: Zondervan, 1986), p. 157.

4. Anthony Campolo, *Growing Up in America* (Grand Rapids: Zondervan, 1989), pp. 112-113.

5. Christopher de Vinck, *Power of the Powerless* (New York: Doubleday, 1988), pp. 11-12.

TALK ME INTO IT

Learn Again to Communicate with Your Child

Trying to communicate effectively with your teen may be one of your most frustrating parenting challenges—yet it has so much to do with how they'll interpret your love and values. Good communication with teens relies on a few proven principles that work!

Karen started in.

Her mom cut her off. "But that's ridiculous! Your dad and I always understand. Why do you always accuse us of not understanding?"

Karen's eyes filled with tears. Everything went silent.

"We'd like to hear the rest of what you have to say, Karen," I interjected. Karen began again. Her mom broke in with a rebuttal. We were getting nowhere.

Finally I asked Karen if I could speak to her mom alone for a moment. She agreed.

"Darlene, I believe what you have to say is valid, but Karen needs an opportunity to share what she believes as well. Let's allow her to talk until she is completely finished. Maybe if she finds us willing to listen, she'll feel we understand. Right now we need to show her we are receptive to listening. Let's give her ample opportunity to complete her thoughts out loud."

Darlene agreed, but assured me that she had heard all of this before and it was nonsense.

We invited Karen back in and began again, for the third time. The conversation started to get somewhere.

Nothing frustrates parents and teenagers more than the challenge of communication, yet nothing means more to the task of passing on faith and values. It's not unique to this generation or this culture. It has always been a major point of contention.

MARY WAS IN A panic. Joseph was downright ticked off. Still adjusting to the dimness inside the temple, Joseph spotted Him. They rushed toward Jesus, who had just finished answering another question asked by the men crowded around him. Mary pushed her way into the middle and grabbed Jesus' arm.

Ushering Him away from the group, she scolded, "Why did you do this? Your dad and I have been worried sick about you!" She squeezed His arm a little tighter.

"That's one incredible kid you have there, ma'am," one of the men shouted after her. She kept walking straight toward Joseph. "He knows more than *we* do!" the man continued, his voice echoing behind them.

Back out in the afternoon heat of the temple courtyard, Mary loosened her grip. Jesus turned to his parents and questioned, "Why were you looking for Me? Don't you know I'm supposed to be in the temple?"

Mary and Joseph stared at Him blankly. *What in the world is He talking about?* Joseph wondered.

Mary looked down at the smooth block of stone where she stood. She didn't fully understand, but she knew He was trying to communicate something significant. All she could do was hold His thoughts in her heart. (Read this story in Luke 2:41-52.)

SILENCE THAT SCREAMS

Good communication between adults and teens isn't easy to achieve. In fact, many families have given up. One study showed that American parents spend less than fifteen minutes a day talking with teenagers. Of those fifteen minutes, twelve are devoted to schedules and chores and only three minutes are used for personal exchange. At the same time, adults are deeply concerned about their inability to communicate with teenagers.[1]

Every summer I take a group of excited junior high kids on a trip through California. They're a wild, funny, rowdy, exasperating, wonderful bunch. (We call ahead to warn local residents that we're coming!)

By way of two cheap walkie talkies, both van drivers attempt to keep in contact with each other. But the walkie talkies never really work that well. There's someone else on our channel, or there is too much static, or it sounds like the other person is talking with marbles in his mouth. The worst case is when the vans get separated by too much distance and we lose contact with each other altogether.

Communicating with teenagers can be like that. Two distinct parties—each coming from his own perspective, each having his own agenda—are trying to get something communicated, but are encountering a lot of static. Frustration wells up, kids stop listening, parents talk louder, teenagers explode, and adults clam up. The worst scenario? Both sides begin to drift farther apart. The distance cuts off communication altogether. The lines go dead.

In his excellent book, *The Friendship Factor,* author Alan Loy McGinnis shares this quote that underscores the problem:

> The fundamental complaint of young Americans . . . does not refer to the hypocrisies, lies, errors, blunders and problems they have inherited. It is, instead, this: That they cannot talk with grown people . . . I have come to believe that the great majority of our kids have never enjoyed an intimate friendship with even one grown person. Why not? When you ask that, you get one answer: Their efforts to communicate with us are invariably and completely squelched.[2]

Communicating with teens is a painstaking art. Many people would rather not be bothered. However, those who are willing to try are generally rewarded with friendship and openness over time. It's that friendship with you that will change a kid's life . . . and yours.

What is required is a willingness to concentrate on the basics. Every time an adolescent opens his mouth, an opportunity emerges. And bonds can be strengthened.

CALM DOWN AND CONNECT

I use what I describe as a "calm down" approach to establishing communication with teens (because I often find myself getting uptight with them). The letters C-A-L-M D-O-W-N create an acrostic that can be easily remembered. These are the kindnesses that nurture communication with adolescents:

Create an atmosphere of acceptance.

If it's true that dogs can sense when we're afraid of them, it's equally true that teenagers can sense when we don't accept their thoughts and feelings as valid. "Atmosphere" seems like a rather ethereal idea, I realize, but it's as real as the world we live in. It's created through small gestures—putting down the paper, easing the pace, looking at the one speaking, smiling rather than frowning, unfolding the arms, nodding as a signal of understanding, relaxing the stance, listening quietly.

When it comes to the difficult task of understanding and communicating empathy to an adolescent, I know of no better example than Christ Himself. He is our empathetic High Priest. He comes to our side. He hears our case. He enters into our plight. He feels our pain. He models our possibilities. In essence, He treats us the way we ought to treat those teens who are trying to talk to us:

"For we do not have a high priest who is unable to sympathize with our weaknesses, but we have one who has been tempted in every way, just as we are—yet was without sin. Let us then approach the throne of grace with confidence, so that we may receive mercy and find grace to help us in our time of need" (Hebrews 4:15-16).

Often, we feel that we can't *accept* what a teenager is saying because we *disagree* with what he or she is saying:

> The key to real communication with young people is the readiness to listen and care about what they say even when we don't agree. Let's face it. Listening is easy when teenagers parrot our beliefs. The hard part is accepting their right to argue, disagree, and speak out against our tightly held views. If we really want open communication with our teenagers, we cannot belittle any of their opinions. They are testing not only *our* reactions but *theirs,* too. And our responses determine, to a large degree, the kind of relationship we'll have.[3]

We actually *can* communicate acceptance without implying agreement. "I can understand your feelings." "There are times when it really seems like God is unfair." "I've felt that way before too." Responses like these communicate a lot of acceptance. Once a person feels like his feelings have been accepted, he is much more inclined to consider another perspective.

Allow for expression.

Based on what we've just discussed, this point may appear repetitive. If so, let it be reinforced. It's that important! The number one complaint among the teens I speak with is that their parents don't give them enough time to express themselves. By the same token, the number one complaint among their parents is that teenagers don't listen to what *they* are trying to express.

So often, expression is squelched at the hands of impatience, busyness, or sheer exhaustion. At the same time, teens need a quiet platform on which to verbalize their thoughts and feelings. In fact, when they're allowed to do so, many of their conflicts are sorted out without our saying a word.

Jumping in with other perspectives too quickly will usually be met with resistance. After all, the person sharing hasn't had ample time to make himself understood, and until he feels understood, he won't be open to trying to understand what you have to say.

JIMMY'S AGITATION AND INABILITY to listen for long in our youth group has remained about the same. (He chews his pencil so loudly during our prayer time that it sounds like a crackling fire!) Fortunately, during the last couple of years his small-group leader has hung in there with him despite his disruptiveness, or tries to at least. One night the noise hit an all time peak and Jimmy was asked to leave the group. I took him for a walk outside and the cold night air seemed to settle him down somewhat.

"I'll bet there's a lot going on in your mind, Jimmy."

He didn't respond. "Go ahead. Lay it on me. Tell me what you're thinking. Believe it or not, I really do care. In fact, I promise I'll shock you with how much I care."

Gradually, over the next half hour, Jimmy opened up a little, and then a little bit more. I said next to nothing the whole evening.

Elaine caught my arm as I was leaving the Saturday night service the next week. "I don't know what you said to Jimmy last Wednesday night but it sure made an impact on him. Thursday he told me some of what you shared with him."

I'm thinking, *What? I didn't say anything!*

"He is so excited about the youth group," she continued.

I never really did get a chance to tell Elaine how little I said and that what I did say was anything but profound. In reality, Jimmy just needed to do some venting. He needed an ear. He needed a few nods, a smile, a firm hug, a "Yeah, I know what you mean."

Ideas, even poor ones, improve with discussion. Problems untangle themselves during dialog. Much is accomplished in a quiet room with an understanding listener. Receptivity to whatever your teen wishes to express is the plow that will till the soil of his or her own heart, and allow for the planting of your ideas and insights at the right time.

Listen with intensity and interest.

Not long after Jimmy and I had that walk around the church, he ended up sitting next to me at a beach barbecue. "You know," he said, without taking his eyes off the flames, "I really wish I could talk to my parents. But they never listen. When my mom's around, she's cooking or on the phone or getting ready to go somewhere. If I hang around, she just barks out orders."

"And what about your dad?" I asked.

"He never really talks to me. The only time he says much is when there's a game on TV or he's mad at me for something." Jimmy paused. "He's mad at me a lot."

I have a confession to make: I'm guilty. The following has happened too many times in the past. A young person comes in and begins talking. I'm in the middle of something at my desk. I give them about half of my attention as they are speaking, and the other half is spent glancing down at my papers or straightening things up. What if, instead, I had given them my full attention? Imagine what it communicates to adolescents when papers on my desk appear to be more important to me than their concerns.

At times we're not able to stop immediately what we're doing and redirect our attention. When that's the case, we can drop things just long enough to hear them initially. Then, looking them right in the eyes, we can patiently explain the nature of our dilemma at the moment and set up an alternate time when they can have our undivided attention. This affirms their importance and still allows us to move ahead with whatever is bearing down on our schedule at the moment. It allows us to be completely plugged in to them once the pressure has eased off.

Listening is actually a golden opportunity with teens. If they'll talk to us, it usually means they like us. Listening is a perfect way of affirming them and setting the course for an even stronger relationship. If we cut them off by interrupting them or talking too much ourselves, we miss out on our opportunity altogether. Chances are they haven't heard a word we've said anyway, so it accomplishes little to interrupt them.

I've come up with at least ten good ways of *blocking* dialog. (I've tried most of them to make sure they work!)

1. Preoccupy your mind with other thoughts.

2. Interrupt with comments.

3. Make judgmental or evaluative remarks about what is being said.

4. Maintain a defensive or hostile stance toward the speaker.

5. Display shock at what is being said.

6. Glance at distractions.

7. Dissect words and miss the intent.

8. Provide quick-solution answers.

9. In your mind, rehearse your responses while the other person is talking.

10. Fold your arms and frown while they're talking.

For some reason, listening is the single act that most closely resembles the "magical solution" we'd all love to discover about relationships. When people are sincerely listened to with patience and understanding, it's almost as if some amazing power takes over and calms them down, makes them more reasonable, allows us to be heard later on, and provides a bridge that can span even seemingly insurmountable relational chasms.

<u>M</u>ake a point of trying to understand.

The old cliche "It's the thought that counts," definitely applies here. Even when we don't understand, the willingness to, or lack thereof, comes through loud and clear.

A couple of years ago, Lori and I took ballroom dancing lessons with a few other couples from our church. It was a scream! We'd watch the instructor, then walk through the motions. The music would start, and with the grace of a gorilla I would step on her feet and turn what should have been "poetry in motion" into a manic game of twister. It wasn't that I didn't understand the instructions, and I definitely knew what I was doing wrong. The problem was that my legs had a loose connection with my mind. I was just slow at pulling it off. Most of the time Lori caught on to the steps before I did, and, as is her style, she'd walk through the routine with me until I worked it out for myself.

Understanding is like that. Often our first tendency is to evaluate, correct, scold, remind, and to generally slip into a mood of irritation until the other person gets things straight. From our perspective the solution seems clear; it usually appears easy. But at the time, what's called for is a plodding patience that attempts to see the situation from the perspective of the other person.

When we do understand, we need to communicate that. When we don't understand, we must communicate that we are trying: "From what you've said, I'm beginning to see why you're angry. Let's talk about it some more. I sure do care about how you feel." Simple statements like these speak volumes of compassion and understanding, even during the process of clarification.

Diffuse tension with appropriate humor.

I once heard of a father who placed a sign in his front yard that read: "For sale, one set of encyclopedias—never used. Teenage son knows everything!"

While true humor will never seek to belittle another or capitalize on sarcasm, adults who succeed with teenagers know how to laugh—a lot. They're able to see the humor in themselves and in everyday situations. They lessen tension, make others feel warm and understood, and have the ability to get through difficulties and pain with a minimum of stress. I've met Christians who were no longer able to see the humor in life. I feel sorry for them. They're missing out on one of God's greatest gifts to humanity.

To be sure, there are times when humor only creates anger, and rightfully so. No one likes to feel as though they're not being taken seriously when they *are* serious. What we're talking about here is taking *ourselves* less seriously. Not being quite so uptight. Not communicating by our words and attitudes that this point of conflict signals the end of the world as we know it.

Moments before Lori and I were married, the officiating minister met with me in a small room for prayer and a few last words. Being a pastor myself, I anticipated what he would share. I expected an admonition such as, "Respect her with humility," or possibly, "Remember to keep Christ at the center of your home." Putting his hand on my shoulder, he said with a smile, "No matter what, keep the laughter alive. Have fun. Really enjoy her. If you can keep the journey fun, much of the rest will fall into place." You know what? That pastor was right. Lori and I have attempted to keep the fun in our relationship, and have enjoyed seven years of terrific marriage.

The same thing applies to living and working with teens. The process can quickly appear too daunting for laughter. Yet, when we genuinely see the more positive side, the lighter side of it all, the hilarity of many issues can provide a little grease for the machinery of communication. Even in the midst of conflict, a little appropriate humor can help ease the pounding in our heads, and help us to resolve the matter at hand.

Open your own heart.

Author Larry Richards discusses four patterns of communication that adults typically use in responding to teens. While all four have their place, our tendency is to use the first pattern most of the time. However, it's the fourth pattern that is the most effective in many situations.

Pattern #1: Advice Giving— This communication pattern expresses the idea, "I've got the answer, now do what I say." It implies that the teenager is weak or unable to think or act on his own. It is often demeaning.

Pattern #2: Reassuring— This response can imply that you have more insight into the problem than the one living through the situation. It also may imply that the situation is no big deal and that it's illogical to be unsettled by it.

Pattern #3: Understanding— This method is generally more helpful than the first two patterns. It communicates that, "If it's important to you, it's important to me." This approach produces affirmation rather than condescension.

Pattern #4: Self-revealing— This style not only invites the other person to come closer, but moves you closer to that person, too. It states, "I'm human too. I share your experiences and feelings about life." It's a touchable stance that searches personal experiences in order to locate common ground. It strengthens both the listener and communication in general.[4]

"My parents never talk about it," is the response I often get when the issue of sex presents itself. Remember Randy? His mom found the magazine stuffed in a dresser drawer. I asked Jean if she or Dennis had ever discussed the topic of intimacy with their son.

"Oh, I suppose we really haven't much. It's harder than you think. The time never really seems right."

"What about the magazine?" I asked. "Could that discovery possibly pave the way for an open dialog between Randy and his dad? What if Dennis were to open up his own heart to Randy and share how he had struggled to keep his own mind pure? What if he were to reveal how he had dealt with sexual temptation—the measures he had taken (such as avoiding pornography) in order to have the kind of intimacy that really satisfies in the long run? The focus could go way beyond the magazine, paving the way to a much deeper and long-lasting conversation."

Jean was open to it. In fact, within a couple of weeks Randy did just that. What began as a threat turned into an opportunity for openness and bonding.

When we reveal our struggles and the methods we've used to cope with them, teenagers are given a model for coping as well. If we refuse to acknowledge our own fitful journey through a complex world, we deprive our kids of the opportunity to see how difficult problems and overwhelming temptations can be resolved and overcome.

So often we feel as though an acknowledgement of failure or of some personal weakness will undermine our effectiveness. After all, our goal is to model positive behavior, isn't it? To reveal weaknesses, we feel, may work against the positive image we want to maintain. While the "super-adult" motif may work with children when they are very young, teenagers generally aren't impressed. They know we can't possibly always be right. They also see our weaknesses (often better than we do). To claim omniscience is ridiculous. To hide basic struggles purposely is futile.

I'm not suggesting that we go into gory descriptions of all our thoughts and sins in the name of honesty. That's not necessary, and can even be cruel. Openness simply means a willingness to reveal failures at appropriate times, to personally identify with the struggles of another, to empathize because of a pool of shared experience. That requires humility, which comes across in the language of transparency.

As long as we're on the issue of openness, it's worth mentioning how crucial it is for us to be honest about our mistakes. When we're wrong, we need to say we're wrong. It's healthy for everyone involved. If we maintain that we are right, even when it becomes obvious that we're not, teenagers immediately come to the conclusion that we cannot be trusted—that we must be out of touch with reality. That's logical. Then, when an important issue comes along and we share our perspective, they aren't as inclined to believe us. The past has made them skeptical of our ability to make good judgment calls. They're not sure if we're shootin' straight. We've lost our credibility. The fact is, teenagers don't mind us being wrong half as much as they mind our being unreal.

Work toward solutions with mutual respect.

Nothing is more nauseating to adults than a "know-it-all." Yet we can easily come across that way ourselves. Despite the fact that we may know more about life than the average teenager, we don't stand to make much of an impression by smothering them with our cloak of wisdom. Discovery is synonymous with interest and motivation. Nothing teaches more than the question, "Well, what do *you* think?"

Authors Norman Wright and Rex Johnson point out that while our first tendency is to jump in with suggestions and corrections, it often cuts short the very process we want to see developing. We're so afraid of poor decisions that we don't allow room for teens to learn to make better ones. If we'll relax, step back, and hear our teenagers out, we will be pleasantly surprised to discover that they have resources and judgments for which we may not be giving them credit.[5]

Wisdom is pounded out on the anvil of personal decision-making. When adults take over, the opportunity for growth is lost. Granted, there are times we are required to take back the reins. There are times when teens want, and desperately need, our input. Those are terrific times. But more often than not they really need a harbor. They need a safe place to toss around problems and ideas without any sweeping judgments from us. A question here and a thought provoker there will fan the flame of mature thought without turning on the heat of rebellion.

How can we help them work out their own solutions? Here are a few suggestions:

1. *Work to understand their feelings and the intention of what is being said rather than dissecting words.* We need to allow them time to sort through their feelings out loud. "I try to talk to my mom," Karen told me, "but we always get in this argument about what I said or what she said. I feel like what I *mean* gets lost in the fight. I

know I say the wrong things sometimes, but it's not what I mean."

2. *Give them space to be "emotional" without expecting them to come to a quick solution.* Good decisions take time. Often the path is paved with some sharp rocks. For a teenager to feel angry, depressed, confused, irritated, or despondent is human. The most effective means for getting beyond those hurdles is to feel them being absorbed by another loving human being. As adults we don't need to feel threatened by that process.

3. *Zero in on issues that seem to be key, avoiding tangents.* We can help them define what it is they are trying to say, but we need to do it in a positive way. For instance, let's say it's 4:00 in the afternoon and our teenager comes home in a bad mood. She flops down at the dining-room table and begins raving about the stupidity of Mr. Jones, the math teacher. We ask why she feels the way she does. She talks about how Mr. Jones never grades papers fairly and gives tests that are too hard.

Our first inclination might be to scold her about having such a bad attitude. Another response might be to try to figure out what to do about this imbecile of a teacher. But maybe, just maybe, the teacher isn't the issue at all. Maybe our ticked-off teen has just failed an important quiz and is feeling really bad about it. Shifting blame makes her feel better.

Sometimes, with a few soft questions and a receptive attitude, side issues peel away and the core problem emerges. We need to be sensitive to that possibility and realize that often the first issue or feeling brought up isn't the most pressing one at all.

4. *Respond briefly, rather than becoming engrossed in a lengthy commentary when given an opportunity to talk.* Let's go back to the dining-room table for another look at the school dilemma. Our teen has shown us to a can of worms. Indeed, she has failed a quiz. This is our big chance for a terrific lecture. Shall we let her have it? Should we wax eloquent about the benefits of study, of applying oneself, of spending less time on the phone, and on and on? As hard as it is to resist, our outline probably isn't going to produce a lot. A little support at this point of failure will most likely go a long way toward building a bridge . . . upon which a few well-chosen comments can cross over effectively at the right time.

5. *Make yourself available for further discussion when they would like to talk more.* What if the dining-room table discussion ended with a statement of openness and helpfulness? Something like, "I sure understand what it feels like to fail a quiz; I've failed *my* share of them. Tell you what, if you feel like it, why don't we go over the material together the night before your next one? I'll look it over and make up a couple of mock questions and you try to answer them. Chances are, we can bring that score up next time."

Or, let's say our teen is still steaming about the teacher. "It's *his* fault," she claims. "I *do* study hard. It's not me, it's *him!*" She gets up, slams the chair against the table, and walks off in a pout. At that point our best approach usually is to communicate that we'd be willing to talk more if she feels like doing it later. Just giving that kind of support goes a long way in a teenager's mind, even if she won't admit it openly. Deep down inside, she's glad you're not writing her off, even when she's being unreasonable.

Notice their strengths.

What would happen if negatives did not account for more than fifty percent of our communication? What effect would it have if every prosecution was followed by a praise, if disagreements were interrupted by statements of common ground, if warnings were balanced by words of encouragement to move ahead? What difference would it make in the way teens feel and respond if every correction was countered by mention of something that was handled well? Constant reminders of failure tend to work against improvement.

Robert was on the phone. "We're sick of his lying. We try to trust him but then he lies about something else. He's always got an excuse, and if he doesn't, he just makes one up."

In the past I'd been perturbed by the same thing. On one of our student ski trips, Jimmy "borrowed" another kid's gloves. It wasn't until the end of the day that we discovered who had them. Obviously, Steve, who owned the gloves, was mad. He'd skied all day without them, and his fingers were about to fall off from frostbite. When I was "tipped off" that Jimmy was using them and asked him about it, he claimed he just found them and didn't know whose they were. I knew he was lying. In fact, I remembered asking him earlier in the day if he'd seen Steve's gloves, and he said he hadn't.

Robert continued, "Yesterday he was a half-hour late when Elaine went to pick him up after soccer practice. He claimed the coach detained him. So I called the coach today and, sure enough, the coach had nothing to do with it. All the boys had been let go at the same time—on time. He was just messing around with his friends."

"What did you do," I inquired.

"Oh, I don't know *what* to do," Robert confessed. "I got pretty mad. I yelled at him. We grounded him like we always do."

"What would have happened to him if he'd just been honest and told you he was carousing with his friends?" I asked.

"I'd have killed him! He knows better than to keep his mother waiting like that! What does he think we are—his servants?"

I asked Robert if I could talk to Jimmy about it. He agreed that I should. The next chance I got, I approached Jimmy with the problem. In the course of our discussion, Jimmy said, "My mom and dad think I'm a liar. They tell me I'm a liar. They treat me like a liar. So, I guess that's what I am." He looked at the floor.

"Is that true? Do you lie to them sometimes?" I asked. He was silent.

I continued, "Jimmy, I've lied too. Sometimes it seems like an easy way out. The problem is, in the long run, you lose trust. You're going to want a lot of trust in the years ahead." I knew what he was thinking—that telling the truth about his failures would get him into a lot of trouble, and that by lying he at least stood a chance of sidestepping repercussions for the misbehaviors that were never discovered.

When Robert and I spoke the next time, I suggested he talk to Jimmy about the matter again. "Consider letting Jimmy know that you *don't* think he's a liar. Talk to him about how much you *want* to trust him. Think of some ways to increase his freedoms when he does tell the truth, even if he's blown it, and point out to him the connection. In other words, make it easier for him to tell the truth. No matter what, affirm your belief that he can be trusted and that you plan on trusting him. Ask him to live up to it."

As with most change, the results were anything but immediate. For a long time I didn't hear any more about it. One evening I saw Robert at church and asked him how things were going. "We're affirming his good points a lot more" he answered. He lowered his voice and added, "I'm trying not to get as angry when he screws things up. Daniel, I think it's helping. I told him I was going to be working at trusting him and asked him if he'd help me by being as honest as possible. I promised him that if he'd just be honest about things, any punishment he receives would be a lot less than if he lied about it. It's going a lot better now."

Strengths are strengthened by affirmation. Weaknesses tend to become more ingrained by the same process. In many ways, teenagers become what we expect them to be. When we communicate trust, hope, and admiration, we actually bolster confidence and a willingness to fulfill our hopes.

IF YOU BELIEVE IT, SAY SO!

Of all the things we want to communicate, most of us would agree that at the top of our list comes *values*. We want to talk about God and what's right, and how our faith impacts life. But it's hard. We get busy. We get tired. We're always patching leaks in the dam. We're not sure just what to say. We doubt their receptivity. It's hard to find the time and the place and the words to bring discipleship home.

Despite our struggle, God planned for communication about issues of faith to originate within families. That's where values are most readily adopted. God made it clear that He wants parents to verbally share their faith and values with their children on a daily basis: "These commandments that I give you today are to be upon your hearts. Impress them on your children. Talk about them when you sit at home and when you walk along the road, when you lie down and when you get up" (Deuteronomy 6:6-7).

According to studies carried out by Search Institute, most families regard issues of faith as being "very important" to them. Of those surveyed, 97 percent claim to have some type of church affiliation. But get this: The teens in the survey were asked, "How often does your family sit down together and talk about God, the Bible, or other religious things?" Forty-two percent say this never happens; 32 percent say these topics are discussed once or twice a month; and a mere 13 percent say they are discussed once a week.[6] When it comes to matters of faith, it's often very quiet on the home front—a *deadly* silence.

I've asked adults why matters of faith are not discussed at home and have grouped their responses into five common complaints:

"I would, but I just don't know what to say."

For some reason many of the parents I speak with feel as though discussions of faith are somehow in a different category than everything else. It's as if there is something hindering them from just being relaxed and natural in sharing whatever spiritual issue or insight is on their heart and mind.

Have you ever known anyone who sells Amway products? I had a friend in college who did. She brushed her teeth with Amway, she washed her clothes with Amway, she supplemented her diet with Amway, and she took stains out of her carpet with Amway. You couldn't be around her for more than an hour without the distinct impression she was CRAZY about Amway. Whether or not you liked or used the stuff, you knew *she* did and that she would die for it. Being around her made you at least wonder what you were missing.

What if our faith in Christ meant that much to us? If He has *really* redeemed our lives, given us purpose, made us royal heirs to his eternal throne, wouldn't it stand to reason that we'd be more than a little excited? Wouldn't that inner thrill come across to our teens? Wouldn't it make them want it too? Our task is to maintain a relationship with the Lord that will allow us, and even inspire us, to speak up and speak from the heart.

Even when we have maintained a genuine personal walk with God, putting what we honestly feel into words can be difficult. The exciting part is that it always gets easier with practice.

"We tried, but it didn't work."

Usually the "try" was some method of formalized family devotions. With conflicting work schedules and a lack of interest by family members, the practice has, in most families, been dropped. With all of our modern time-saving conveniences, we haven't managed to slow down a bit. In fact, the pace has accelerated in most American homes. There is such a plethora of options competing for our time that unless family discussions are considered top priority, they will get lost in the shuffle.

A common mistake is to think of "devotional time" as something rigid and highly structured. It doesn't appear Christ felt that way. In fact, much of the time He spent interacting with His disciples on issues of faith could be classified as very informal.

During the summer months I often take groups of guys camping near the ocean. One evening last summer, we set up our tent and then went for a walk along the shore. After a good sand fight, we sat down to watch the waves. The atmosphere became a little more contemplative, so I ventured, "Hey, let's all try to think of one thing that happened to Christ and His disciples when they were at the Sea of Galilee."

Immediately, light bulbs went on all over the group. "There was the time Peter walked on water," one of the guys responded. "What was the story?" I asked, giving him an opportunity to exercise his memory. He proceeded to paraphrase the event. Each one in turn identified another event from the Bible. Finally, I asked them to share which incident they most identified with in their lives right now.

One said he felt like he was one of the disciples with Jesus when Jesus was asleep in the boat. "I feel like life is so crazy, and I wonder where God is when all this stuff is happening to me." Another boy said his relationship with Christ was really strong but his friends didn't understand him at all. He identified with the story where Christ ordered demons out of a man and sent them into a herd of pigs, angering the locals who owned the pigs.

When we returned to our campsite, I had the guys take out their Bibles, read the passage they said they identified with, and write the date next to the story. "That's cool," one remarked. "When I read this in the future I'll remember when we talked about it." What started out as a simple question turned into an hour of devotions. The possibilities for informal devotional times are limitless. We need only look around us for opportunities to bring the Truth into our daily lives.

"Everyone is apathetic . . . I just can't hold their interest."

There was a time on the prairie when the Bible was the most exciting thing on the shelf. There were no television sets, no Nintendos, no phone calls, no stereos to entice us. But that world will never be again. Our culture is action-packed. Many families feel that devotional times—discussions of faith and values—can't compete.

I keep finding that, despite the technological competition, very personal conversations about how the Bible relates to real needs can and do get attention. The key, however, is making it relevant and tangible. A good devotional guide can be of great assistance.

While I've been studying the Bible for years, hardly a day goes by that I don't turn to some type of study aid for help in making passages clear, understandable, and more interesting. This is where a good family-oriented devotional guide can be beneficial. There are countless good ones to choose from that can be adapted to the ages and stages of those in your family. The same is true for a Sunday school class, or a small-group Bible study, or a one-on-one discipling relationship.

While using a guide can be helpful, guard against allowing it to overshadow the personal dimension of a faith discussion. For it to work, we must internalize the truth, then share our thoughts very personally with those listening. The trick is to get discussion going through the use of provocative, well-thought-out questions. Once the discussion is underway, the attention level is normally high for a while.

I ONCE SAT IN on Randy's small group. His studies at the Christian college he was attending were paying off. He had prepared well. His material was well-organized, his outline precise. He began; the students were with him for the most part. He continued; they now looked a little distant. He went on; they began to doodle. He neared his conclusion. By this time all of them were in another world. He ended, and his students looked relieved.

"What's wrong with them?" Randy asked as we walked outside together. "It's like this every week." I probed Randy's thinking for some possibilities. Together we concluded that he didn't give them much of an opportunity to interact with the material. It was shared, as in a lecture, rather than discussed. It was packaged rather than provocative. "Jab them!" I suggested. "Goad them with questions. Get them thinking. Play the devil's advocate. Make 'em squirm. Get them to argue your points a little."

Randy approached his next lesson with our discussion in mind. He jabbed, and they responded. "It was hard to get them talking at first. But after we got going, I couldn't get them to shut up! I never did get through my lesson."

"But do you think they walked away thinking? Did they learn?" I asked.

Randy was convinced they had. They probably gained more than he realized.

"I'm not sure I can answer their questions."

Many of us fear looking uneducated or unspiritual if questions are asked that we can't easily answer. No one can anticipate the questions a fifteen-year-old may come up with, but by maintaining an attitude of humility, our lack of knowledge can lead to a little research and better understanding. Those questions can provide a springboard for discussion and further digging. It's the questions my students ask that keep me going back to the Word for answers. All of us have an aversion to saying "I don't know." However, when that response is followed up by this promise: "I'll help you find out," the ball gets rolling and a biblical conversation can turn into a treasure hunt for the Truth.

Every year I sit down with my staff and we assess the needs of our Student Gathering at church. We brainstorm ideas and arrive at plans for our teaching agenda. Invariably, the students themselves want to study the book of Revelation. Every year we teach on it in some form or another, and every year I am forced to decipher the book's imagery. It isn't easy. One thing has kept us coming back to it, though. The students are *interested*—even if we don't have all the answers. Mystery doesn't bother them half as much as it bothers me, and I am forced to conclude that it's OK to talk about passages that are steeped in controversy and shrouded by our limited understanding.

"Educating my kid is the church's job. We take him every week."

While most parents I speak with won't actually come out and say this, they live it week in and week out. There seems to be a mistaken undercurrent of belief that the church can, or at least should, do it all.

The church can provide a push once or twice a week, but the pull that will create an appetite for faith must come from a regular diet of Truth provided by those people teenagers trust the most. Youth pastors, counselors, and others who work to direct young people, have a monumental task before them as it is. Like attempting to teach a one-year-old to walk, a half-hour lesson once or twice a week simply won't cut it. The child needs a daily opportunity to stretch his legs and find encouragement in the process.

We don't need to have all the answers, nor must we reserve our faith discussions for "sanctified" times. The reality of God and His workable plan for life should be interwoven into every moment of every day, and discussed from one heart to another, complete with partial understandings and uncertainties.

NOTES:

1. Mary Susan Miller, "How to Talk to Your Teenager," *Good Housekeeping,* October 1989, p. 251.

2. Philip Wylie, quoted in Alan Loy McGinnis' book, *The Friendship Factor* (Minneapolis: Augsburg, 1979), p. 113.

3. Jane Norman and Myron Harris, *The Private Life of the American Teenager* (New York: Rawson, Wade Publishers, Inc., 1981), p. 7.

4. Larry Richards, *Youth Ministry* (Grand Rapids: Zondervan, 1971), p. 139.

5. Norman Wright and Rex Johnson, *Communication: Key to Your Teens* (Eugene: Harvest House, 1978), p. 100.

6. Merton P. Strommen and A. Irene Strommen, *Five Cries of Parents* (San Francisco: Harper and Row, 1985), pp. 133-34.

RELIGION THAT RELATES

*Today's Churches Need to Adapt
to the Needs of Teens*

Alot of teenagers are bored to death of church. The fact is,
it doesn't have to be that way. When parents and youth
workers discover how to involve teenagers in all aspects
of church, a new dimension of motivation is unleashed.

We stepped out of the taxi into thick, humid air and made
our way up a cut-stone walk toward a tiny house that was nes-
tled among banana trees and flowering tropical foliage. Spread
out across the small yard were scattered folding chairs, and card
tables supporting smoldering hibachis and bowls of fish stew.
Thai people were milling about, all talking in their native
tongue, laughing, drinking, and chewing on bits and pieces of
food. "Sit down, sit down!" our host greeted us. "Welcome to
Thailand," he announced, loud enough to gather some glances.
Everyone nearby smiled and nodded warmly. We were seated.

"Here, you'll love this!" An older Thai gentleman who was
seated at our table handed Lori and I a skewered piece of beef
off the hibachi. As instructed, we dipped it in peanut sauce and
chomped down on the leathery meat. Zowie! My mind raced
while my face remained neutral. I turned to Lori, whose face
was already bright red. "Hot stuff, eh?" I whispered. She smiled
and quietly cleared her throat. Before long we were each presented with a bowl of fish soup. Pieces of fish that looked very
lifelike floated in a murky, sizzling, spicy sauce. I nearly lost it.

The birthday party continued. The man who had invited us tried to include us in everything going on, but everything going on was well beyond our comprehension. Everyone spoke Thai. We sat and smiled. They played Thai birthday games. We sat. Everyone sang in Thai. We smiled. They all took off their shoes before entering the house. We were well inside before realizing we were the only ones with shoes on. Embarrassed? You bet!

The Buddhist altar, with its candles and red glowing bulbs, seemed strange. The faded photos of national Thai statesmen seemed like odd decor for the living room. The symbols, smells, sounds—we may as well have been visiting Mars. Fresh from our Western world, we didn't understand any of it. This was Culture Shock 101. Never had foreigners felt more foreign. It was obvious that we didn't fit in. As much as these kind people tried, and as much as *we* tried, the cultural gap was a huge one, and difficult to bridge.

Those images often come to mind when I see a teenager sitting in church. Formal hymns, recitation of creeds, happy-looking people all dressed to the hilt, religious symbols, a statue of a man on a crossbeam who has blood dripping from His wrists, side, and feet. Think of the hurdles teenagers must overcome when visiting the local church. Many churches seem just downright strange to people who don't go to church. Some seem rigid, almost hostile. Others are characterized by liturgy and Greek symbols and archaic chants. Some are filled with moaning people who are waiving their hands in the air while a sweaty preacher shouts and pounds. Others are quiet as a morgue.

All of those church cultures can be valid and understandable once you meet the people inside. Usually there are good reasons for the way people gather to worship. To those people, it all makes sense. But for the average American teen, it's another world. A world that often seems too bizarre.

So where does this lead us who are on the *inside* of the church? I believe it urges us to lower as many walls as possible. The youth in our nation need to find a church environment that is sensitive to *their* culture, just as the church of the past has adapted to fit our own. Church must become "user friendly" to teenagers if it hopes to show them the Gospel and nurture their faith. It's not unthinkable to even question, "Can today's church work for a new generation? Can it make any difference?"

THE IMPACT OF CHURCH

While nothing can compare to a truly Christian home where relationships are strong, a church where teens feel they fit in is a powerful resource for moral development. In many cases a Christian home environment just isn't an option. In others, teens come from Christian homes where family relationships have disintegrated and little spiritual nurturing is being transmitted from one generation to the next. In families where parents do provide a foundation of Christian training, the need is to have those values reinforced through the lives and examples of respected others outside of the home.

Nearly every study conducted over the past forty years has shown that the more an adolescent attends church, the less likely he or she is to become sexually active. Those researchers have concluded that religion is one of the most consistent and powerful influences on adolescent sexual behavior.[1]

So how do we create a church culture that draws and keeps teens? What kind of church experience will lead teenagers toward genuine faith and lifestyle? First off, the church must become tolerant of teens.

CHURCH SHOULD BE LIBERATING

Diversity is God's trademark. It is His brand on humanity. All of us in the church must come to grips with the fact that similar values based on the absolutes of God's Word are going to be fleshed out differently in everyone. Sweeping judgments about a kid's inner life, based on outward indicators, often lead to a bad call. God never intended to "cookie cut" humanity, and He doesn't do it with Christians. Unfortunately, Christians do it to other Christians and all of us suffer for it. There is great loss when we do not allow for differences in personal expression of shared faith and values. With every personality comes a different display of faith.

I'd like to tell you a true story about an eighteen-year-old guy named Chris. He was rowdy and as rebellious as he should be at that age. At the same time, when we met, Chris was experiencing revival in his spiritual life and he and I became good friends. After a period of discipling, and a lot of loving and listening, Chris's gifts blossomed and he began leading a small group of younger teens. He was incredibly effective at drawing them to the Savior. He went on to become a paid intern, and, finally, the director of our church's junior high program. He's one of the finest Christian men I know. But Chris has one glaring flaw in some people's estimation: He has a pierced ear. And for that, some people didn't want him in leadership.

Let me tell you a true story about another boy. His name is Greg, and he used to be on staff in our high school department. Everyone who knows Greg would agree that he has a phenomenal gift of evangelism and a heart for the lost. He's now away at college preparing to go into full-time missionary service. I can honestly say I've met few people I admire more than Greg. He's really got his act together — except for the fact that he's got long blond hair. Too bad for Greg. According to some churchgoers, he ought to be disqualified.

We want young people to love and obey God because they'll be happier if they do. We have in our minds a picture of what love for God and obedience to His Word looks like. We expect our teenagers to match up to that picture. When our expectations are met, we feel successful. When they aren't, we're disappointed and often upset with them.

If somehow we could put that picture of a "good Christian" on an overhead transparency, we'd find that our expectations are divided into two overlays. We start with a picture of a person— maybe our thirteen-year-old daughter, or a kid in our Sunday school class, or a nephew in another state. Then we lay a set of expectations over the original transparency. This first set is clearly biblical. It's right that we have these expectations. There are arrows directed at various parts of this adolescent, describing God's will for his or her life:

- Be honest. *(Colossians 3:6)*

- A rebellious attitude is bad. *(1 Samuel 15:23)*

- Don't steal. *(Exodus 20:15)*

- Love others as yourself. *(Matthew 22:39)*

- Don't be a gossip. *(2 Corinthians 12:20)*

- Keep sex within marriage. *(Hebrews 13:4)*

- Be self-controlled. *(2 Peter 1:6)*

- Don't murder people. *(Exodus 20:13)*

- Don't hate others. *(Leviticus 19:17)*

- Be filled with the Spirit. *(Ephesians 5:18)*

- Help those who are in need. *(1 Corinthians 12:28)*

- Don't get drunk. *(1 Corinthians 5:11)*

- Seek humility. *(1 Peter 5:5)*

. . . And so forth. All of them are biblical.

Then there is a second transparency we lay over our picture. This one contains another list of expectations, but these are borne out of our own personality, age, cultural background, perspective, denominational ties, unfulfilled dreams, social customs, and a host of other factors. They combine to form our opinions about the way "Christian" people ought to think and behave. This second overlay may include points like these:

- Men should have their hair cut above their collar.

- Rock music, no matter what the lyrics, is bad.

- Neatness is akin to godliness.

- You should be dressed up for church.

- Good Christians don't dance.

- A true Christian would never smoke.

- Wearing black clothes means you're a Satan worshiper.

- Staying out past midnight will lead to trouble.

- Fat people are all gluttons.

- Rich people are selfish.

- Poor people are lazy.

- Christians in other denominations are suspect.

- Men who wear earrings are sissies.

- Too much makeup means you're a loose girl.

. . . And on and on and on the list goes. Write up your own list. We've all got one.

All those preferences and opinions aren't necessarily *always* wrong. But, they're *ours!* They may not be God's, and they may not be true in another place and time. There are many qualities we desire to see in a young person that are not clearly spelled out in God's word.

It's so easy and natural to slip an item from list two (my opinions) into list one (God's directives). After all, if it appears that God feels the way I do about this or that, then my opinion is obviously right. We tend to put words in God's mouth that He's never uttered, and pen ideas into His Book that He never wrote.

Conversely, it's sometimes convenient to let a clear command from list one (God's directives) slip into list two (my opinions). "So I'm a gossip. It's not that big of a deal." Or, "Fudging on my taxes isn't so bad. There's no way they're ever going to know, and it's not like they don't take enough as it is."

Daily life has a way of extracting what we believe, not what we say we believe.

A church that impacts teens has got to have a really good handle on its lists and expectations. Biblical is beautiful. Bias is legalism. More teens have left the church due to a confusion of the two. When the personal-preference list becomes canon, teenagers are quick to detect it. And for good reason, they don't buy it. Even worse, they throw out the biblical along with the biased.

I appreciate a story Jay Kesler has shared about a time he approached a "strangely dressed" teenager. Jay honestly thought the kid was wearing a costume and asked him about it. The kid responded by saying, "This isn't a costume, it's my clothes!" Grabbing Jay's tie, he continued, "Why do you wear that?" "Well, uh, I wear ties," Jay explained lamely. The student fired a barrage of questions: "What's their function? Why do you wear them? Are you a conformist? Don't you have any character, any integrity? Can't you be yourself? How come?"[2] The point was well made.

While living in Ghana, West Africa, as a teacher in a Bible College, I learned that Ghanaian culture, as well as its expression of Christianity, is very different from ours. How?

• They dance in church.

• Men walk down the street holding hands with their closest friends.

• There is no public display of affection between men and women.

• People go to church in what we would call a bathrobe.

• All women go to work; they just take their babies with them.

• It's appropriate to drop in at someone else's home any time, unannounced.

- In normal weather conditions, it's a sign of unfriendliness to close the front door of your home.

- Church services may last three to four hours.

Those cultural expressions may not wash in America in this day and age. But they work just fine in Ghana. God is just as pleased with their social distinctives as He is with ours. And it may be that He is just as pleased with some of those teen-culture distinctives that bother us so much.

In the same way, when a church makes major issues (or worse yet, spiritual issues) out of personal preferences, they are inadvertently stealing steam from the real issues of life and godliness. It is tragic when exterior conformity is used as a gauge of spirituality. When churches do that, they are virtually slitting the spiritual throat of their younger members. Rigid control of nonessentials such as hair style, choice of clothes, or the use of certain musical instruments in worship, will only create unnecessary distance. Then when the real issues, God's issues, need to be addressed, the teenager will have already written the church off as being legalistic.

Just what are those real issues? God's issues give primary focus to *character*. It's in developing character qualities that a tone for all of life's choices will be set. Certainly God's commandments given in Deuteronomy 5 form a base for principled living. And beyond those, the New Testament elaborates and defines what pleasing God looks like. Ministries to youth must make concepts such as these the focal point of their teaching.

"Love the Lord your God with all your heart and with all your soul and with all your mind . . . . Love your neighbor as yourself" (Matthew 22: 37, 39)

"So I say, live by the Spirit, and you will not gratify the desires of the sinful nature" (Galatians 5:16).

"But the fruit of the Spirit is love, joy, peace, patience, kindness, goodness, faithfulness, gentleness and self-control . . ." (Galatians 5:22-23).

"Let us not become conceited, provoking and envying each other" (Galatians 5:26).

"Carry each other's burdens, and in this way you will fulfill the law of Christ" (Galatians 6:2).

"Since, then, you have been raised with Christ, set your hearts on things above, where Christ is seated at the right hand of God. Set your minds on things above, not on earthly things" (Colossians 3:1-2).

"Therefore, as God's chosen people, holy and dearly loved, clothe yourselves with compassion, kindness, humility, gentleness, and patience. Bear with each other and forgive whatever grievances you may have against one another. Forgive as the Lord forgave you. And over all these virtues put on love, which binds them all together in perfect unity" (Colossians 3:12-14).

"Devote yourselves to prayer, being watchful and thankful" (Colossians 4:2).

"Finally, brothers, whatever is true, whatever is noble, whatever is right, whatever is pure, whatever is lovely, whatever is admirable—if anything is excellent or praiseworthy—think about such things" (Philippians 4:8).

Many in mainline churches balked at the "Jesus People" movement of the 70s. It just didn't fit within the comfort zone of many established Christians. At the same time, a research team of psychologists and sociologists from the University of Nevada made a study of the movement. In an effort to understand these followers of Christ, the researchers spent time among them in one of their communal villages. Reporting on their experience in *Psychology Today*, they wrote, "All of us who interviewed members came under such pressure that we felt the need to withdraw at least once a day in order to reaffirm our own world views."

T. George Harris, then editor of *Psychology Today*, stated, "Each time [the research team] called in after a visit, we asked them if any of them had been converted to the movement. At least one of the researchers had trouble hanging on to scientific certainty while he lived day and night among the vibrant, born-again Christians."[3]

Wow! That's exactly what the church is supposed to be doing. Granted, we will all use differing methods, but when the fragrance of Christ is permeating a group of people to that extent, we should be applauding, not throwing rocks.

During my years in seminary I worked as an assistant to the high school pastor at the First Evangelical Free Church in Fullerton, California. At the time, it was in style to have what we called a "tail," which simply meant to let your hair grow longer in one place at the base of your hairline. Mine hung about four inches below my collar, while the rest of my hair was short. I really liked the look but it drove some of my seminary buddies nuts. Although we were all good friends, it really bugged a few of them.

One afternoon I was sitting at my desk in the church office when our Senior Pastor, Chuck Swindoll, walked in. We began talking about all sorts of things. And then the issue of my hair came up. I wasn't really sure how he felt about it, but I knew Chuck well enough to know he wasn't one to be too swayed by insignificant issues. He asked me if I got any flak at school for having my hair the way it was. I told him I got a little, but it was worth it. I explained that, in part, because of my hair the teens we worked with felt they could relate to me. They felt comfortable around me. He smiled. Turning to leave, he simply said, "Good. I like it. Keep it." And he walked out.

Our task, then, is to major on the majors and to set a clear agenda for what we hold to be true. That agenda must come straight from Scripture. The other agenda, those personal preferences, is fine to have around as long as they are labeled as such and never confused with what God has set forth clearly.

THE CHURCH THAT HELPS TEENS . . .
HELPS ADULTS TOO

Every Sunday I watch the procession. A parade of nice cars with tinted windows passes slowly through the church parking lot. One of the cars will stop and the back door will swing open. There will be a brief interchange of information and a kid will bounce out of the car. The door will slam shut. The car will continue its glide from the parking area. Next car. Next door. Next kid. No adult.

I asked some parents whose children are now young adults what they did to instill values and influence behavior. Their responses revealed that their involvement at church had a great deal to do with the success of their efforts. I also found that the attitude of that religious experience was one of grace.

Larry and Terry Keelin are parents whose children are now in their twenties. The two of them are preparing to begin second careers as missionaries. Terry Keelin noted:

What really worked was being involved in a church, all of us, and being involved in the youth activities. We knew the friends our kids hung around with. We also let our teenagers know that there are consequences to all their choices—but that we would love them no matter what choices they made.

I SAT ACROSS THE table from Joe and Darlene. Karen and her sister sat with us, each wearing a strained look of obligation. I had trouble enjoying my burrito. Darlene kept up a fine monolog: "I just can't believe what people do. They come and sit in church like prima donnas and then go out and live it up all week. The church is full of them! Oh, and do you know what Carol Sydell told me yesterday? She says the Fosters aren't getting along at all. Yet, Mr. Foster is still teaching that sixth-grade boys class. I really think the church ought to do a better job of looking in to those kinds of things, don't you, Pastor Daniel?"

All was quiet except for the munching of tacos. I looked at Karen. She was studying a piece of lettuce on her plate. Her sister was watching another family in the booth across the aisle from us.

I looked at Darlene, who was still waiting for my answer. "Uh, well, yeah, I guess so," I muttered. All I could think about was the training that was taking place at that very moment. Little did Darlene realize that she was inadvertently teaching her girls to be critical of others and to slander those who are a part of Christ's body. She didn't mean to do it, I'm sure, yet she was modeling the very character that she would not approve of if seen in someone else.

. . ..FOSTERS AN AUTHENTIC IDENTITY

One of the factors enabling the Israelites to maintain their faith in God was that of a strong identity. They knew they were God's chosen people, and children growing up in the Jewish community knew it immediately. "For you are a people holy to the Lord your God. Out of all the peoples on the face of the earth, the Lord has chosen you to be his treasured possession" (Deuteronomy 14:2).

The same was true for the early Christians. With persecutions rampant, first-century believers huddled together for safety. They helped each other survive, and interdependence was critical to survival. Their identity as Christians could cost them their lives so no one in that culture "toyed" with the idea. They either were or they weren't. Once they crossed the line of faith, it was an identity that they lived and breathed twenty-four hours a day—or for which they died.

Paul wrote to the early church, "For he chose us in him before the creation of the world to be holy and blameless in his sight" (Ephesians 1:4). Peter added, "But you are a chosen people, a royal priesthood, a holy nation, a people belonging to God, that you may declare the praises of him who called you out of darkness into his wonderful light" (1 Peter 2:9).

There it is: a vivid identity, a self-concept that defined how they would live their lives, a perspective on personhood that has been blurred by a modern, somewhat "Christianized" culture.

While our culture is anything but truly Christian, the masses consider themselves "Christian." But this is a label that doesn't really apply in many cases. It's a word with a weak definition. It's a way of feeling better about the hollowness inside. And people who go to church aren't necessarily any different. If "Christian" is a label for these people, rather than an all-engulfing identity, then the same will be true of the churches they fill. Those churches will be branded "Christian," but they will lack the backbone to fill the billing.

Along these lines, I've found teenagers to be significantly more perceptive than adults. If the church is breeding hypocrites, teenagers can spot the problem pretty quickly. If the teaching is dry and impractical, they can detect it in one sitting. If the worship is mundane and irrelevant, they will call it what it is.

Unfortunately, many churches have become like corrupt weigh stations along the freeway of life. They're a place to get checked off as being "spiritual," regardless of the truth. Many Christians in American culture find it soothing to their guilty souls to glide through a routine church service weekly, monthly, or just on holidays, in order to "rubber stamp" themselves "APPROVED," even when spiritually they're dead. The syndrome is passed on to our teens.

> This generation . . . has grown up in a society that has taught them that faith is a private matter and should not interfere with the public areas of our lives. Because of that, many young people believe that faith is only a *part* of life, not something that influences all of life. The result is that . . . students can come to church, be very vocal and involved in their faith, then walk out the door and ignore their faith all week long, *and see no contradiction in their behavior*.[4]

That kind of church-going is lethal to true faith. It's like replacing the bandage on skin cancer once a week. It does nothing for true spiritual healing, and provides our young people with ammunition to expose our hypocrisy and "blow off" our religion. If they're intelligent, they probably will. They'll see that it is nothing but a mask, and they'll tire of the lie. The answer is found only in true discipleship. It starts with us as adults. We must begin by faith to accept Christ and His Lordship as our lifeblood — the very center of our being, the core of our personality. And secondly, we must carry the concept into our churches.

To be authentic doesn't mean we have all the answers. Quite the opposite. The natural journey toward a personal faith is fraught with doubt. Yet, when teens uncover inconsistencies or express doubts, we sometimes react with demands that the Truth, as we understand it, be adhered to. No "ifs," "ands," or "buts." God said it. You believe it. That settles it. Authentic faith, however, is not threatened by questions. In fact, in an atmosphere of dialog and searching, true belief is fertilized. The Gospel can easily withstand soul-searching doubts.

If the church is going to reach teenagers, it must be truly Christian. In other words, it must be calling its people to honest faith in God through Christ. It must be accepting of honest questions and people who are very much in process. It must have as its primary mission a commitment to help believers become authentic disciples. In short, it must prepare people to walk with God the other six days of the week.

. . . WILL BE RELEVANT

Michael Pountney, Rector of the Church of the Ascension in Montreal wrote insightfully:

> "I love Christianity, it's the church I can't stand." Many have been turned off by the taste of organized religion they've gotten within the four walls of that Victorian red brick on the corner of First and Main — the one with the leaking roof and damp bathroom that seems to reflect the age and weariness of the congregation within.[5]

Most teenagers feel that "religion," as they conceive it, is losing influence in America. According to the Institute for Social Research at the University of Michigan 65 percent of high school seniors in 1980 said religion was "very important" or "pretty important" in their lives. Only 56 percent agreed in 1990. Researchers saw the same drop in church attendance. Forty-three percent of kids in 1980 attended worship services every week. In 1990, only 30 percent attended.[6]

Is it really any wonder that teenagers find church boring? Dennis Miller, founder and president of Church Youth Development, Incorporated, published a report stating that 65 percent of "evangelical" teens never read their Bibles and 33 percent of them feel that religion is "out of date" and "out of touch."[7]

Jack Sims, a consultant in Placentia, California, is attempting to wake churches up to their need for relevance before it's too late.

> It's OK for churches to change the container that religion comes in. Think about what a traditional church is like. An old person greets you at the door and hands you a mimeographed bulletin. You sit in an uncomfortable pew and stare at the back of someone's head. You sing 400-year-old songs and listen to a 20-minute talk about theology. Then they ask you for money . . . If you stay for the coffee hour afterwards, it's like going to someone else's family reunion![8]

When we question why our teens are not more interested in church, we may not need to look much further than the methods we're employing to communicate a life of faith. Think about it. How many times can a young, active mind endure ritualistic services and repetitious creeds which require little or no thought to recite? Teens wonder about the idea of a God who enjoys such mindlessness.

Church must relate to real people—people who have jobs, live in a modern, fast-paced world, face sins of a technological age, and who are groping for answers to contemporary problems. Too often the church has become "the mighty fortress" *instead* of God. Many who ascend the stone steps find nothing more than a hollow cathedral with words and lives to match.

Effective ministry to a new generation naturally requires updated methods — methods that reflect the uniqueness and personality of any new age and culture. As is always true, openness to change allows us to rethink what we are doing. It prompts us to reevaluate whether our methods are accomplishing God's desire for the church at any given time in history. That evaluation process is important not only so that we'll adapt to meet the needs of young people, but it is crucial for the very life and continuance of the church.

Sarah really stood out when she attended our church service on Sunday mornings. In fact, she stood out so much that she quit coming. In the youth group she was fine, but in the church service she felt awkward and out of place. Besides that, she couldn't understand the language used in traditional hymns, nor could she understand many aspects of the message. But Sarah isn't alone. All of us on the pastoral staff began sensing that an increasing number of people in both our congregation and community were looking for a different kind of "worship culture."

So, we started a Saturday night service that featured a band instead of an organ. The worship and prayer time was a little longer and the message from our senior pastor a little shorter. And the atmosphere was definitely less formal. It worked. Now there is a service that has adapted to the needs of a large group of our people. Including Sarah.

What we did isn't necessarily what any other church should do. It's just what *we* did. Every church needs to assess the pulse of its people—even its younger people—and invent appropriate ways of meeting those needs.

. . . WILL BE ROOTED

During Jimmy's junior year his attendance in our youth group began to taper off. He'd show up every other week or so, and when he did he often had a story about a concert he'd been to or some really cool speaker he'd heard at another church. We spoke together about it one afternoon when he dropped by my office.

"I've been going to Holy Cross a lot lately. They have a basketball league there and, well, you can't be in the league unless you go to church there."

"Makes sense to me," I replied. "What's the teaching like?"

"Oh, I don't know . . . the same, I guess."

"Well, wherever you go to church, Jimmy, just make sure they're really teaching from the Bible," I added later in the conversation. "Get fully plugged in and become a contributing part of that Christian community. If you don't find it there, then come back. You know we really love you and want to see you grow in your faith. Your faith is the most important thing.

"And Jimmy," I added, "church should be a good time, but the bottom line is getting to know God better through His Word. In the long run, that's what will keep you going. All the concerts and speakers and ball games are great, but ultimately you need to ask yourself, 'Am I in a place where the basics are the most important—basics like worship, instruction from the Bible, community life with other believers, reaching others with the Gospel, and service to God?' Look for those, Jimmy, no matter where you go."

For the next couple of months Jimmy went back and forth. He'd show up, then he'd be gone again for a week or two. One Sunday he arrived and took me aside. "I'm back," he announced. "I looked for those five things you talked about and they weren't there. This is where I want to be."

Underneath the programs that exist in any church or youth group there must be an abiding and unchanging commitment to the truth of God's Word and its outworking in the lives of the believers who gather there. We're back to bedrock. Teaching must be rooted in something that will not and cannot change with time or circumstance.

Why is the Bible so critical? Why stress its teaching above all else? Because Scripture, and only Scripture, provides the authoritative operations manual for moral relationships.

Without that absolute, society offers little help. Programs come and go. Opinions fluctuate and fail. And most importantly, admonishments about behavior lack authority when they are not grounded in God's authority. Moral restraint without moral absolutes is illogical and unreasonable in a self-oriented culture.

You may recall the highly publicized, brutal rape and beating of a woman jogger in New York's Central Park in April of 1989. When questioned in court, the kids who committed the atrocities appeared almost surprised that anyone could fault them. After all, society scorns moral absolutes. The media repetitively encourages us to live out our impulses without restraint. Without defending their abhorrent behavior, we've got to admit that these guys were acting on the moral messages they'd been raised on. Bible-based teaching reverses that trend. It claims there are absolutes that are worthy of our attention and adherence.

While accounts of teenage delinquency are a dime a dozen, adolescents are actually far more open to issues of faith than they will be at any other period in life. I am constantly amazed by the hunger and enthusiasm teenagers have for the Word of God when it is presented as a workable and reliable witness to absolute Truth. They really want answers to their problems. They want to know why they're here and why God is there, and what to do about it. They have reached an age of cognitive reasoning, of searching for what is true. At no other point in life are they as able or willing to evaluate and internalize that Truth. Later on as adults, much of that search will diminish. Defense mechanisms against change will be firmly entrenched. When presented with fresh insight that is illustrated meaningfully, the Bible can stop rebels in their tracks.

Many teens are frustrated with the lack of biblical teaching in their churches. Youth groups must go beyond the fun and games (which are great) and provide direction straight from the mouth of God through His Word (which is essential).

. . . FOSTERS CROSS-GENERATIONAL RELATIONSHIPS

A major factor behind adolescent acceptance or rejection of Christianity is the bond between teens and adults who work in youth ministry. Psychologist Garry Powell is quoted as having said, "I feel it is almost impossible for a Christian teenager to make it today without the support of an adult friend." Earl Wilson elaborates, saying, "Young people need to link themselves to strong Christian values, but this link is not always provided by their parents. There are too many hooks in parent-teen relationships which prevent the young person from taking advantage of the adult perspective."[9]

With the emergence of adolescence comes branching out. New emphasis is placed on what others think and believe outside of the home, and new ideas are screened through the grid of teenagers' upbringing. At this stage, other authorities can dramatically influence the acceptance of values. A church which realizes this potential will create programs designed to enhance relationships between mature Christians and teens.

At Mission Hills Church we began by talking to a group of young adults about the potential impact of forming discipling relationships with the teens who attended church there. We named our group the "Mission Hills Student Gathering," and started out with about fifteen junior-highers and twenty-five high school students, dividing them into small groups, each with an adult who was willing to spend time with them. That was over five years ago. Today there are forty older teens and young adults discipling more than 200 active teenagers.

What has kept us going has been visible evidence that, over time, many teenagers assume the values of their small-group leaders. The approach really works. No wonder Christ was so partial to it. With probably more than two million Jews living in Palestine during the first century, Christ chose *twelve* to work with! Christian values are more caught than taught, and "catching" happens best in the context of a life-on-life relationship between an adolescent and an older person.

Nearly half of the students in the Gathering are from homes where there is little or no spiritual input. These students are utterly dependent on the relationships that are built within our program. For that reason, the power of a discipleship ministry among teens must not be underestimated. Too many youth ministries are relying on mass meetings and glamorous personalities up front, while kids are dying for relationships that model the Truth. Why is that? Probably because discipleship, over the long haul, is a thousand times more difficult than presenting the Gospel and letting it go at that.

. . . PROVIDES FOR SIGNIFICANT INVOLVEMENT

Even though my relationship with Jimmy was good, his attendance at church began to diminish again during his senior year. When he did come he seemed a little bored. We talked some about it but he never really expressed why he was missing a lot of the time. One Friday we met at the fitness center to lift weights together after school.

As we made our way through a series of workouts, we talked. It became apparent that Jimmy felt "fed" by the group but that's where it stopped. So I popped the big one. "Jimmy," I ventured, "have you ever imagined yourself being a leader in our group?" He smiled and looked embarrassed.

"I'm not good at speaking in front of people," Jimmy responded.

"What do you think you are good at?" I asked.

"I don't know, I haven't really thought about it."

"Well, I think you're really working at a strong relationship with the Lord. Others in our group look up to you. You get along well with people. Would you consider being an assistant in a junior high small group? It could prepare you to be a leader in our junior high program."

Jimmy was observably shocked that I wanted him in leadership but he began to think about it. Within a couple of months he was helping out with a core group of six seventh-grade boys. What's even more amazing is the amount of patience he displays with those guys. He understands when they squirm, poke holes in their outline, and count ceiling tiles—he's barely beyond doing those things himself. Jimmy began moving from a "feed me" mentality toward one that focuses on feeding others—and in the process he found a new level of maturity unfolding.

Dr. Robert Laurent conducted a significant study of 400 teenagers and identified ten reasons for declining interest in religion among teens. One reason stood out as predominant over the rest. What was it? Simply this: a lack of opportunity for church involvement.[10]

Many teenagers can't see how they're supposed to fit into the church. As long as they can conform culturally to the church, and are willing to come, sit down, and listen, they're welcome to attend. But church often isn't structured to *involve* them. So they lose interest.

In Laurent's study, the lack of opportunity for church involvement proved to be the number one reason teens eventually reject religion. Over seventy-five percent of the youth who demonstrated a general alienation from religion indicated that the church's failure to take them seriously and include them in significant roles is the major cause of their estrangement. Laurent maintains that our idea of adolescence as a "waiting period" betrays our lack of understanding. Teenagers need to be challenged, needed, excited, trusted, and given opportunities to participate. When we deny adolescents an immediate role in the church, we're unwittingly prolonging spiritual immaturity and selfishness, belittling their sense of self-esteem, and incapacitating them in their natural desire to help others.[11]

In our youth Gathering, one group of students is responsible for working up skits and short one-act plays. Another group helps to lead music and evenings of worship and sharing. There is a club for students who wish to help set up our room, make posters, decorate for parties, and contact new people. Another group of high-schoolers assists with our junior high program. There are "Class Servants" who organize activities and programs. Students are active in serving at church dinners, teaching Vacation Bible School classes in the summer, running backyard Bible clubs, helping with the elementary-grades classes, and counseling fourth-, fifth-, and sixth-graders at camp. And every summer we send some students overseas for missions work. Almost every regular attender is in some form of leadership. We learned long ago that we "use 'em or we lose 'em."

Sometimes they don't come through. They do shoddy work. They're not motivated. But that is only sometimes. Much of the time their competence is surprising. Usually, with a lot of encouragement and a few successes under their cap, they'll keep on working and improving. All the while faith is taking on dimensions of reality. They see how it applies to daily life.

. . . EMPHASIZES TEACHING FROM LIFE EXPERIENCE

Students form their beliefs out of the substance of their experiences. Whereas adults are prone to accept something as fact simply because they are told it is so, adolescents look at their life experiences and then choose to believe the things that match with what they've observed to be true. If a "fact" doesn't square with their experience, it is immediately suspect.

For instance, you may tell an adult "God loves you" and show it to be true based on biblical information. He will more readily accept the idea of God's love based on that information than a teenager will. This is especially true if that teen has come in contact with God's people who are unloving. His experience tells him that it can't possibly be true that God is loving when those who follow Him are so unloving.

"It's so hard for me sometimes around other Christians," Sarah explained. "I sort of expect non-Christians to be cruel. But how come so many people who call themselves Christians aren't anything like Christ?"

"I've never had a good answer for that," I told her. "I think it has something to do with what Paul described in Romans, chapter seven. We're always battling the old life."

"But it seems like some of the people in our church aren't battling it at all," Sarah objected. "They don't act like they're trying. They gossip and put people down and talk about all the material stuff they have . . . but they act like that's cool—like it's OK to be that way."

I knew what Sarah felt. I've felt it about myself. I so easily talk righteousness while I so quickly walk the opposite. Love is easier said than done. I explained to Sarah about some of my own inconsistencies and how I often gloss over them and ignore working on changing them. She took it in but obviously had a hard time processing it. To Sarah, Truth is evidenced by what she sees, and she's looking for Truth in the lives of the people at church, regardless of what they say is true.

Just like Sarah, most teenagers are more impressed by what they see and experience than they are by what they hear. The ramifications of this are many. For one thing, our teaching must involve life-related examples and experiences in order for doctrine to be decoded, and for faith to be fleshed out and felt. Dennis Miller, president of Church Youth Development Incorporated, points this out:

> Since students determine the value of truth by their experiences, the Church must begin to utilize life experiences more in teaching. We must reestablish the credibility of what we teach by demonstrating that the power and presence of Christ make a visible, measurable difference in our lives—not just in how we talk or think but in how we live.[12]

Church programs implement this reality by providing teaching situations that involve students in real-life scenarios such as role-playing, creative debates, service projects, asking students how they would counsel a friend in a particular situation, having students produce a video which captures them living out or simulating a certain positive behavior, and so on. The creative alternatives are limitless.

A few years back I was teaching a series for our students on the importance of all people in the church. My staff initiated the idea of a "Young and Retired Party." Our teens invited guests who were over fifty-five to a banquet the students themselves hosted. In a very tangible way they were able to get to know some older Christians and thereby deepen their love for them. Both the students and our senior guests loved it, and more was taught about acceptance of others at that banquet than in my entire series of talks. We need to *do more* and *talk less.*

JESUS GOES TO CHURCH

Although the idea of the Christian church really began in an upstairs room in Jerusalem, Christ provided the model for church life while He walked among us. His was a band of believers who grew to embrace faith on a daily basis. His was a method of leadership that transformed dead religion into a living relationship.

Christ's ministry on earth, as recorded in John's Gospel, reads like a really good "church life" manual. A glimpse inside that world—a brief walk along the Sea, a moment to stop and watch Him with His disciples—will teach us a lot about passing faith on to teens in the church.

Acceptance — He met them on their turf.

Christ's own approach toward mankind was one of humble acceptance. He became incarnated. He became one of us in order that He might reach us. In Paul's words, "[Christ] made himself nothing, taking the very nature of a servant, being made in human likeness" (Philippians 2:7).

Early in Jesus Christ's ministry we find Him sitting on the edge of a dusty old well talking to a woman. Not only was she a woman (taboo!) but a Samaritan woman (double taboo!). Worse yet, she was a Samaritan woman who had a reputation for being, well, "loose" with the men in town (triple whammy!).

When His disciples arrived on the scene, one would have expected them to come unglued. Christ was, after all, bulldozing His way across all sorts of religious and cultural boundaries. But they didn't fall apart. They just stood there with dropped jaws. John 4:27 records the scene for us: "Just then his disciples returned and were surprised to find him talking with a woman. But no one asked, 'What do you want?' or 'Why are you talking with her?' " And why didn't they ask these logical questions? Simply because they had learned from personal experience about the amazing acceptance Jesus showed toward people. They had themselves been the beneficiaries of His willingness to set form and style aside and reach out to people—*all* people.

One thing has been true of teenagers in every generation. They are dying for acceptance beyond the home front. That has never been truer than it is right now. With so many teens disillusioned at home, many of them are turning to the church for love. When they do end up associating with the church, we'd better be ready to receive them with open arms.

Christ-centered relationships with teens must reflect a great deal of sensitivity to where teens are coming from and a willingness to accept them at that point. In short, it requires a real servant's attitude. Christ hung out with smelly fishermen and shrewd tax collectors. He stepped over to our side of the tracks. If God made that kind of sacrificial adjustment in dealing with us, how much greater is our obligation to humble ourselves and reach out to teenagers, even if they make us uncomfortable.

Realistic — He made the Truth livable.

Over time, Jesus had a few men who wanted to be with Him. That was His goal. In the second chapter of John, right at the beginning of Christ's public ministry, we find Him at a wedding feast (on their turf). And who was standing right there next to Him? You guessed it: those men. Right there, He began to reveal who He was through the miracle of providing wine for the banquet, and His disciples were watching every minute of it. "This, the first of his miraculous signs, Jesus performed in Cana of Galilee. He thus revealed his glory, and his disciples put their faith in him" (John 2:11).

There is no stronger witness than that of revealing the character of God through action. Those men saw first-hand that God was in Christ, and they believed. We, as Christ's representatives, now have the opportunity of showing the character of Christ alive in us. Those who watch us will be drawn to Him as well.

I wish I knew who wrote this, but it's so good and right, I wish it were engraved on church doors across our nation:

> I simply argue that the cross be raised again at the center of the marketplace, as well as on the steeple of the church. I am recovering the claim that Jesus was not crucified in a cathedral between two candles, but on a cross, between two thieves . . . on a town garbage dump, at a crossroad of politics so cosmopolitan they had to write His title in Hebrew and in Latin and in Greek; and at the kind of place where cynics take smut and thieves curse and soldiers gamble, because that is where He died and that is what He died about. And that is where Christ's men and women ought to be, and what church people ought to be about.

Friendships — He brought them home.

It may begin by giving teenagers a ride or providing them with a racquetball partner. Come through at their points of interest, and appreciation will develop. Trust will be built. At first they won't reciprocate much, if at all. It can seem like a real one-sided friendship.

A common pitfall of relating to teens is expecting much reciprocation. Relationships still remain something of a mystery for adolescents. Usually, other-centered thinking doesn't develop quickly or easily, which can really annoy adults who attempt to build a mutual friendship with a young person.

"Turning around, Jesus saw them following and asked, 'What do you want?' They said, 'Rabbi, (which means Teacher), where are you staying?' 'Come,' he replied, 'and you will see'" (John 2:38-39).

Spending time with those men was the glue that bonded their relationship and allowed for "discipleship" to take place. "After this, Jesus and his disciples went out into the Judean countryside, where he spent some time with them, and baptized" (John 3:23). The very first Christian summer camp! I imagine they found some good swimming holes, enjoyed fishing together, had some food fights, wrestled with each other, stayed up late talking, and slept under the stars. They became friends, and all the while, the disciples *watched* Him.

By now, you've learned much of Jimmy's story. All that pent-up energy and need for belonging is being funnelled into love for others. As I look back, however, I remember so many times that I wanted to throw in the towel. For five years I invited Jimmy to go with me when I had errands to run. I provided him with taxi service when he needed to get places. I had him over for meals. Took him camping. Went to the beach. You name it, we did it together. For years I would have told you my chances were slim to none of ever living to see the payoff.

I remember occasions when I would clear my schedule to do something with him and he just wouldn't show up. No phone call. Not even an apology the next time we'd meet. Other times, when we would get together, he would be so moody or self-absorbed that I felt my being with him was a waste of time. More than once (in fact, many times) I wanted to just forget him and walk away.

Only two things kept me going. One was prayer. Every time I prayed for Jimmy, I felt a real desire to hang in there with him. Secondly, from time to time I'd see some tiny sign of growth. Now when I see him, he's got a little tribe of seventh-graders in tow. He's so crazy, they like him. And when they can't sit still, he understands.

FRIENDSHIP IS THE BEST MINISTRY METHOD

I could recount to you other stories of guys I've really poured myself into who didn't respond at all. For a period of time we were close and then gradually they'd drift off. Phone calls, letters, invitations, personal visits—all these produced nothing. They just wanted out. So I had to let them go.

It's comforting to know we're not first. There were thousands who came alongside the Savior and who, for one reason or another, simply shook their head and walked the other way: "From this time many of his disciples turned back and no longer followed him" (John 6:66). They had that choice.

Remember the ruler who asked Jesus what it would take to acquire eternal life? Jesus told him. In fact, the text tells us that Jesus looked at him with real love. But after the requirements of discipleship were spelled out, he refused the offer.

Relationship-building with teenagers will require more time and patience than we've ever invested in anything else. Unless we're locked into Christ ourselves, we'll find our spiritual resources running dry very quickly. Once we drift from dependence on the in-filling of the Holy Spirit, it's only a short time until our personal reserves give way to impatience, frustration, and loss of vision for what we're supposed to be doing. To make things worse, our example to those watching us becomes a negative one.

There's a humorous, but insightful, story about this guy who painted white stripes down the highway for the Department of Transportation. The first day, he painted five miles of stripes. On the second day, he painted two miles; the third day, 576 feet; and the fourth day, only 180 feet. The boss called him in and asked him, "Are you sick?" "No," the painter replied. The boss then asked, "What's the problem?" The painter said, "I just keep getting farther and farther away from the bucket." Effective discipleship only happens when those in leadership are "close to the bucket," when we ourselves are walking close to the Lord and being replenished by time spent with Him in prayer and meditation on His Word. If we don't, we'll be running ourselves ragged but accomplishing less and less.

Reflection — He made them think.

Jesus had just finished feeding four thousand people on a hillside from a young boy's lunch box. The disciples were feeling pretty secure in this whole relationship. But Jesus knew that His demonstration of God-given power was not sufficient to prepare them for the onslaught of social pressure they would be facing. So He put it to them:

"Who do people say the Son of Man is?" He inquired. The disciples could deal with that one. "Some say John the Baptist; others say Elijah; and still others, Jeremiah or one of the prophets." There: Case closed! A nice, safe overview of the options. Then came the challenge: "But what about you?" Jesus asked. "Who do you say I am?" That was the zinger. Now the mental machinery was humming. Jesus had given them a dilemma. He had made them think. It's a great story. Read it for yourself in Matthew 16.

That kind of tension, or quandary, is necessary for moral development. It's the injection of disequilibrium that will lead to stronger personal convictions. In his excellent book, *Teaching Techniques of Jesus*, author Herman Horne quotes Dr. W.P. Merrill, who beautifully captures Christ's intent while on earth.

> His aim, as the Great Teacher of men, was, and ever is, not to relieve the reason and conscience of mankind, not to lighten the burden of thought and study, but rather to increase that burden, to make men more conscientious, more eager, more active in mind and moral sense.
>
> That is to say, He came not to answer questions, but to ask them; not to settle men's souls, but to provoke them; not to save men from problems, but to save them from their indolence; not to make life easier, but to make it more educative. We are quite in error when we think of Christ as coming to give us a key to life's difficult textbook. He came to give us a finer textbook, calling for keener study, and deeper devotion, and more intelligent and persistent reasoning.[13]

This process is often overlooked in our Sunday school programs, as well as in our pulpits. Christ used it to great advantage, and the disciples were prodded and provoked to think beyond superficial replies.

The flourishing churches of the future will be the ones which have responded with flexibility toward the culture of their younger members, without compromising their biblical integrity. They will be the churches who prize their young people—who invest heavily in them, knowing that tomorrow's church depends on those kids.

While church can assist in the process of growing toward godliness, it's not a sure cure. It doesn't wipe out all our diseases. We're still sinners. All of us have a hard time appropriating what we know to be true. The narrow path is rough and bumpy. There's lots of sidetracks. Numerous valleys. No one said it was going to be cheap or easy. No one said there wouldn't be some major disappointments. But the rewards for making the effort are great.

NOTES:

1. Ronald L. Koteskey, *Understanding Adolescence* (Wheaton: Scripture Press Publications, 1987), p. 98.

2. Jay Kesler, *Ten Mistakes Parents Make with Teenagers: And How to Avoid Them* (Brentwood, Tennessee: Wolgemuth and Hyatt Publishers, 1988), p. 68.

3. Mary W. Harder, James T. Richardson and Robert B. Simmonds, "Jesus People," *Psychology Today*, December 1972, Vol. 45, p. 113.

4. Mike Yaconelli and Jim Burns, *High School Ministry* (Grand Rapids: Zondervan, 1986), p. 66.

5. Michael Pountney, "Who Needs the Church at First and Main?" *His*, January 1985, p.1.

6. *Group*, Oct. 91, "News Trends and Tips," p. 8.

7. Dennis Miller, "Christian Teenagers: They're Leaving the Flock," *Moody Monthly*, September 1982, pp. 11-13.

8. Brad Edmondson, "Bringing in the Sheaves," *American Demographics*, August 1988.

9. Earl D. Wilson, *Try Being a Teenager* (Portland: Multnomah Press, 1982), p.108.

10. Robert Laurent, *Keeping Your Teen in Touch with God* (Elgin, Illinois: David C. Cook Publishing Co., 1988), p.15.

11. Ibid., pp. 15-22.

12. Miller, p. 13.

13. W. P. Merrill, "Christian Internationalism," quoted from Herman Horne's *Teaching Techniques of Jesus* (Grand Rapids: Kregal, 1978), p. 51.

CHAPTER 9

DISCIPLINE THAT MAKES A DIFFERENCE

Learn the Role Your Patience and Forgiveness Play in Changing Teens' Behavior

Reasonable, consistent standards that are enforced within a context of total forgiveness can make all the difference when the reality of failure comes crashing in. So much can be accomplished, even in the midst of failure, if a few key elements are put to work.

The night air was thick with dread as David scanned the horizon. A small silhouette on horseback drew closer as David watched from the balcony. Throwing his cloak around himself, David dashed down the stairwell to the main entryway, arriving as the messenger dismounted.

Seeing David, the young soldier fell to his knees, placing his face to the stone floor. David knew the news would wound him forever. Lifting his head ever so slightly, parched words fell from the man's lips: "My Lord, Amnon your son is dead. Absalom, your son, has seen to it that he be struck down in the field to avenge the deeds he had committed with your daughter Tamar two years ago. Absalom has fled to Geshur. That is all, my Lord."

In silence David stepped away into the darkness and leaned into the wall of the hallway. The bony fingers of regret tightened on David's throat, and he began to cry. He, a man of God, had made mistakes, but now this. His daughter Tamar had been raped by his son Amnon. Amnon had been killed by

Absalom, and now Absalom, heir to the throne, had defected. How could God have let it happen? (Read the story in 2 Samuel 13—15.)

Teenagers rebel. Lives are thrown into havoc. The hearts and hopes of caring adults are shattered. Sin takes its toll on even the best of intentions. David's errors as a father had been great, but so had his suffering. "Picture perfect" kids live only in fantasies. Even one of the most powerful kings who ever lived wept alone over his own children. There are no guarantees.

I'll bet some tears were shed one hot afternoon on a Galilean hillside when the story of the prodigal son was told. His story is our story and the story of our children. Most teens are prodigals, to one degree or another. They're breaking away and, in their inexperience, they're destined to make poor choices. Some of those choices will bring about lifelong scars, like scratched-up trophies for wisdom won the hard way.

WHEN THE HALO SLIPS

The smell of charbroiled hamburgers was hypnotic. Karen and I stood in line, attempting to be patient, but both of us wondering why it wasn't moving faster. The blazing Southern California sun was sizzling the sand, and sounds of the Salt Creek beach crowd filled the air. From where I stood, I could see a group of young people passing a paper bag, taking gulps in turn. It obviously was alcohol. Karen noticed it, too.

"Been to any good parties lately?" I inquired.

"Why do you ask me stuff like that?" Karen shot back with a smirk. "I don't party . . . very much . . . and even if I did, I wouldn't tell you. You'd probably nark on me."

"Yeah," I countered, "and I'd have you arrested and sent to juvenile hall until you're thirty, and I'd make sure your driver's license was revoked and that all of your friends disowned you, too." Karen rolled her eyes.

"Believe it or not," I continued, "I've got better things to do than to keep a list of your sins in my pocket so I can pull it out and show it to your mother when I see her.

"Actually, we're friends, and friends care about friends. I really do care how you're doing. Honest. Between you and me and God . . . and this line of people standing here." Karen laughed.

"OK," she said. "I go to parties now and then. I drink sometimes."

Karen looked longingly past the row of heads, toward the open "ORDERS" window. "I already know that," I said. "How are things with you and God? You did a lot of changing in Mexico City. Do you ever talk to Him?"

"No, my mom does that for me."

"What do you mean?"

"My mom always says she's praying for me."

Teenagers test the limits of their freedom. They try all the possibilities. They question what we've taught them through a broad spectrum of experiments with life. Some of those experiments are benign. Many of them are dangerous.

Why do they do that, we ask? Adolescence is the period of time in which children move from a stage of conventional to principled moral reasoning. In other words, they leave childhood with a strict moral code of right and wrong handed down from adults. They wade through adolescence, all the while developing the capacity to analyze and reflect on what is supposedly true. They become aware of other value systems and behaviors. Now, rather than simply accepting, they are reasoning and questioning the values of their parents and society. This generally has a grating effect on us adults who have grown accustomed to having our dictums accepted without question.

And to muddy the waters even further, they aren't consistent. I have yet to meet a kid who's gone "all bad." Despite what I've been told by some of their parents, I've never met one who is "all good" either. Most teenagers are like chameleons. They change as their environment and whims change. One minute they're a glowing reflection of all you've taught them. The next, they're doing the very things you abhor.

Every now and then my two-year-old daughter gets into our walk-in bedroom closet and has a heyday. She yanks loose various articles of clothing hanging there and tries them on. She'll step into Daddy's huge shoes, or pull Mommy's sun dress over her head. Then she toddles out into the bedroom, garb in tow, to analyze the outcome in the mirror.

Teenagers are doing the same thing with a thousand different behaviors—trying them on, taking them off, seeing what appeals, what hurts, what works. They can be excessively egoistic but just hours later thrust themselves into projects of amazing self-sacrifice. They try on love affairs with the regularity of changing outfits. They're deeply concerned about the environment one second and leaving trash in a parking lot the next. They can be absorbed by materialism one day and ready to join Mother Theresa in Calcutta the next.

Realizing what is going on gives us adults a much greater capacity for understanding and patience during this period of exploration. While we have to monitor what is safe and what is not, we also must leave as much room as possible for the natural process of trying on various adult behaviors.

Obviously, this isn't easy on us. For good reason, we're thrown into a panic when grim news hits home:

"Your son was caught shoplifting."

"I got a ticket, dad . . . for reckless driving."

"Mostly C's . . . and one D."

"Your boss called. They're going to let you go . . . He said you're late almost every day."

"You lied to me!"

Our kids die of embarrassment. We feel angry. We begin to question, *What did I do wrong?*

At this point there is a very important distinction to make between behaviors which seem unusual and those which are reoccurring as habits. Flights of misbehavior often don't indicate that a teenager is "going off the deep end," as he or she may appear to be. Patterns which become evident over a six-month duration are better indicators of a teenager's moral condition than are sporadic divergences. The research conducted in this area indicates that, while most adolescents rifle through behaviors which differ from that of their upbringing, by the time they reach their young-adult years, nearly all young people hold to basic values which were instilled during their earlier years.

Kohlberg conducted a study of older adolescent students in the 1960s. A number of them who had rated as highly moral in high school had become involved in some sort of activity considered delinquent, or less moral, once they were in college. However, every one of those "retrogressors" had returned to a high degree of morality by the time they were twenty-five years old.[1] The point is, young people go through periods of delinquency. But they normally don't stay there. That's the good news. Moral values instilled over the years are reevaluated and, in the process, often are temporarily rejected in order to discover "what is best for me personally." The outcome generally is very positive.

In the mean time, how should we respond? What is appropriate? What, on our part, will instill a sense of personal responsibility without crushing their spirit?

UNDERSTANDING VS. UNDERMINING

Teenagers are desperate to know they are loved even in spite of their blunders. In fact, those mistakes and sins are the litmus test of true love. As I heard a speaker once say, "If you say you love your teenager, he'll put you to the test. He'll spill coke on your car upholstery and then watch to see if you love him more than your upholstery."

"THIRTY-FIVE BUCKS IN tips!" Sarah proclaimed as she poked her head into my office. "One guy left me a five-dollar bill on a twenty-dollar ticket!" Still wearing her waitress uniform, she sat down across from me.

"I really am proud of you, Sarah. How's it going down there? Are people pretty nice to you?"

"Oh yeah, they're fine." Sarah looked serious. "I came by to tell you something."

"What?"

"You know how I've only seen my dad a few times in the last eight or so years?"

"Yeah?"

"Well, he walked into my restaurant today. We talked for a little bit on my break."

"What happened?"

"He talked about his new wife and what was going on with his job. It was cool for a while. Then he said he had been talking to my mom and he'd heard about how I was into drugs and, well, you know, how I almost had a baby. Then he asked me about school and why I had dropped out . . . and he wanted to know why I was working in that 'scummy cafe,' as he put it."

Sarah looked at the floor.

"I couldn't believe he said that. It was like I was so excited to see him, and right off the bat he puts me down for struggling with school and he slams me for my job. He doesn't even know anything . . . " Karen's tear-stained face melted into her hands.

After a minute or so, I whispered, "What did you say to him?"

"Nothing. I just sat there and felt myself starting to cry, so I told him I had to go. He kissed me on the cheek when he left and I felt like slapping him. I get so angry sometimes, I feel like killing him." Tears streamed down Sarah's cheeks. "I shouldn't say that . . . I'm sorry," she added softly.

I handed Sarah my box of tissues. She straightened at the mock apron on her uniform. Looking up at me as a clump of hair fell down over one of her eyes, she said, "Daniel, sometimes I feel like no matter how hard I try, I'm never going to make it. I know I've made a lot of mistakes . . . but all I've ever wanted was for my dad to love me. I don't understand why he wouldn't even try to contact me in all these years."

IT'S CRUCIAL THAT OUR teens know that regardless of what life brings, our love will never change. No matter what. They need to hear that in a thousand ways. They need to be convinced that to our dying day we will love them, even if they fail on every count. They cannot make enough mistakes to keep us from loving them. Are we telling them that? Are we living it?

Adolescents stumble and fumble and mumble their way toward adulthood. Most are adults in the *very* rough. Like a diamond, cutting is a lengthy and costly process. Many of their mistakes are hardly premeditated, and may even occur on the battlefield of good intentions. Clarity of foresight, logical thought, principled judgments, wise reasoning, and mature decisions are (or *should* be) adult characteristics. Adolescents are far from refined. But that's why they're called adolescents and not adults. Understanding that will keep us from undermining them with impatience, comparisons, and criticism during the course of this already difficult maturing process.

Sometimes it helps to step back in time. Imagine some of the fears you had as a teenager. Remember the stresses you felt, the issues you debated, the arguments you flung at the authorities in your life? Think of life, for just a moment, from the kid's point of view.

Usually (but not always) he *knows* what is right. Yet, he has more difficulty than an adult predicting consequences, and an even greater difficulty processing behaviors out of his still somewhat thin layer of convictions. Think about all the social, cultural, and peer pressures working against him. Do you remember the temptations and feelings of rebellion that welled up inside of you for no understandable reason, and the stubbornness that struck when you least expected it? When we take a few steps in their sandals, we generally find ourselves feeling a little more tolerant.

POSITIVE VS. PUNITIVE

Chances are, next to us our teenagers' efforts at adulthood look pretty feeble. They're less punctual, more disorganized, less responsible, more moody, less skillful, and more sinful . . . maybe. In general, however, teenagers are more aware of their shortcomings than adults are aware of their own. Yet adults sometimes become addicted to critical evaluation.

Advancement and improvement hard won can go unnoticed, while errors are magnified for all to inspect. It's a lethal habit.

"MY PARENTS NEVER TALK about anything I do right," Jimmy confided on one of our campouts during the summer. "They come unglued if I do something wrong but never say anything when I do everything the way they want it. It's like they never even notice. Half the time I don't even know what it is they're mad about. But, oh my gosh, if I mess up, my dad goes crazy. One time I left my bike in the driveway and he backed out and smashed it. He grounded me for a month and a half!"

Often, we use our own growth as a standard, as the measuring stick. After twenty, thirty, forty or fifty years we've matured to a certain level. We look at what a teenager is doing, or *not* doing, and we're annoyed. *They're not like us. They're making a mess of things. What's wrong with them?* And how quickly we have forgotten our own fitful journey.

In the face of our own failures we tend to quip, "Oh well, you can't bat a thousand." Yet, for some odd reason, we tend to react harshly to those same failures when exhibited in others younger than us. In 1980, pro baseball player George Brett's goal was to bat .400. His objective was to make an out less than six in ten times. As it turned out, Brett was less than forty percent effective, yet his effort was hailed as phenomenal.[2] Why? Because even though he wasn't perfect, he was good. Very, very good. Why is it that we have such a difficult time seeing all the good, all the successes, of our teens? Much of the time they're not batting a thousand, or even .400, but many are trying hard and hearing little applause for their attempts.

Many studies have been conducted on styles of discipline. Psychologists categorize parental disciplinary styles in various ways, but most of the designations are similar. For our purposes, let's use three which are fairly characteristic of other defined systems as well.

The *authoritarian* style is the "iron rod" approach. Generally speaking, it could be characterized as severe, unsympathetic, impatient, humiliating, and forceful. The *permissive* style could be described as the "Do as you please" method. It indulges, coaxes and bribes, sentimentally wavers, and ultimately submits to the will of the teen. The *authoritative* approach could be described as the "loving discipline" style. Its goal is to maintain self-control, show love, act with tact and gentleness, and yet firmly adhere to set standards of behavior. This system for discipline rises out of verses such as Ephesians 6:4, which reads, "Fathers, do not exasperate your children; instead, bring them up in the training and instruction of the Lord."

Robert Laurent, who discusses these patterns and applies them to parenting, says:

> God has never taken pleasure in forced obedience or blind submission. You must win your teen's affection if you want to impress him with Christian truth. With genuine love and esteem for the dignity of the teen, it is possible for a parent to enlist the will and the reason of a teenager on the side of obedience. When kindness and affection attend them, teenagers respect parents of uniform firmness and unimpassioned control.[3]

Handing out a lot of "thou shalts" and "thou shalt nots" can have a seriously detrimental effect on moral growth. Issuing authoritarian statements to our teens is often our first impulse. However, assistance in reaching a moral decision based on principles of Truth will actually help to strengthen their ability to make good decisions when adults aren't around. When we offer authoritarian solutions, we undermine the natural course of deliberation so necessary to this age and stage of development.

ISSUES VS. INDIVIDUALS

There is a world of difference between communicating "You failed at this" and "You're a failure!" We can handle "I blew it this time," but to feel like "I *always* mess things up," can put us under. A careful distinction must consistently be made between bad actions and bad people. When confronting a problem, the focus of our communication must remain on the issue in question. What went wrong? Why is that wrong? What problems resulted or could result? What should be done to make it right? What could have been done differently? What will be done in the future?

"ACTUALLY, IT'S BETTER WHEN my dad gets mad at me than when my mom does," Jimmy told me one day. "She doesn't yell or anything, she just gets really depressed. She won't talk to me and she looks really sad. Sometimes it goes on for days. Sometimes she's so mad that she won't even look at me for a couple of days."

"How does that make you feel?" I asked.

"Terrible! It makes me feel so guilty. I feel like a total scum. That's when I think about moving out. I wish I could get an apartment with some of my friends."

AS LONG AS A teenager's failure is over an issue, there is hope and renewed determination to change. But when the bony finger of accusation points directly at personhood, confidence is lost—the very confidence needed for change. "Why are you like that?" "Why are you such a failure?" "You're never going to amount to anything if you keep that up!" "How could you be so stupid?" "You are so irresponsible!" "Won't you ever change?" "You're an embarrassment to me!" "God hates people who lie!" Statements like these communicate a judgment of personhood which will shred a young person's self-confidence and ultimately his or her ability to perform in a positive way.

Dr. James Dobson credits William Glasser for helping us to understand that there must be an important distinction made between discipline which leads to constructive behavior and discipline which is focused on punishment and often leads to destructive feelings and behaviors. When discipline is directed at the objectionable behavior and is focused on modifying that behavior, the child can more easily accept the discipline without resentment.

By contrast, Dobson describes punishment as a response that is directed at the individual. It is a personal thrust leveled at the child himself. It's a desire of one person to hurt another. It's an expression of hostility rather than corrective love. As such, it is deeply resented by the child. Rather than having a positive corrective result, it creates guilt and anger.[4]

The purpose of punishment is to inflict a penalty for an offense, whereas the purpose of discipline is to train for correction and maturity. The focus of punishment is past misdeeds, while the focus of discipline is future correct deeds. The attitude of punishment is hostility and frustration, while the attitude of discipline is love and concern. The child's emotions following punishment are fear and guilt, but the emotion resulting from discipline is security.[5]

Guilt is an effective short-term behavioral prod. So we use it. And reasonable levels of remorse are healthy. However, when guilt becomes a primary tool it can be overly oppressive and harmful. Statements like, "You're such a slob. Don't you have any sense of respect? Why are you so lazy all the time?" do little to inspire and do much to deflate motivation.

INDUCTION VS. INCRIMINATION

David Aleshire points out three methods commonly used by adults to modify behavior. The first, *power assertion*, is defined as physical punishment or some other type of force exerted over the child. While these methods can be helpful before children are old enough to reason things out intellectually, by adolescence they are counter-productive in establishing self-discipline. It only leads to conformity as long as the one wielding the whip is within range.

The second method is what he calls *love withdrawal*. This approach involves pointing out how the one at fault has affected others. It is generally characterized by a non-physical expression of anger, or withdrawal of love or attention. This technique also results in immediate modification of behavior, but at a tremendous emotional and spiritual price. It is steeped in guilt which, if overused, can destroy a sense of personal well-being and hope. It fuels anger and leaves lasting images of a parent whose love is conditioned by performance.

The final method Aleshire refers to is *induction*. It appears to be less effective at first. However, it accomplishes more lasting behavior changes. The process of induction asks questions which help a young person evaluate why something is wrong and contributes to their acceptance of responsibility for wrongdoing. It tends to foster understanding of right and wrong apart from external rewards or punishments, a willingness to be honest about failures, and only appropriate levels of remorse.[6]

DENNIS, RANDY'S DAD, WAS good enough to share his ski boat with our students for the weekend. Lake Mead is a sweltering place, even in September, so Dennis and I took a break from setting up camp and sat down at one of the picnic tables.

"Dennis, remember that time Jean found a girlie magazine in one of Randy's drawers?"

"I remember," Dennis said, smiling. "It wasn't one of our finer moments."

Leaning forward on my elbows, I continued, "What I want to know is, how did you handle that? All Jean told me was that you ended up talking to Randy about it and everything worked out great. In fact, she said it turned out to be a really positive thing. What did you say?"

Randy looked out over the lake and shared what he could remember of the conversation. "It's been a while now. I remember we went for a walk and I told him that his mom had found it. In the same breath I assured him that I could identify with his struggle and told him how I, too, had faced those kind of temptations. I remember asking him if he had ever thought about what pornography did to the girls on those pages. I asked him what he wanted most in a relationship with a woman, and we talked a long time about issues like that.

"It's funny now. The thing I remember the most is that by the time we got done with the talk, he was doing most of the talking. He was really concerned for all of his buddies who are into that stuff. He wanted to know what he should do. So, again, I asked him what he thought he should do. He talked about how he wanted to confront one of them that he's pretty good friends with. He also decided he ought to take down a swimsuit poster that was in his room. He felt it just wasn't right. He didn't want his friends seeing it and thinking that he approved of the stuff they looked at and the way they talked about women."

As Dennis and I headed out in the ski boat that day with a kid on the end of our rope, I thought about the countless discipline dilemmas we face. I thought about my own patterns of handling the failures of my students. I had to critique my own methods in light of Dennis' good example.

Many of the students I speak with long for induction as opposed to lectures. While lectures are easier to dish out, they're less effective and more demeaning than questions which prompt the adolescent to verbalize his own understanding of failure and resolve to change. Ultimately, we must come to terms with the fact that what our teen says will make a much greater impact on his or her thinking than what we say.

FORETHOUGHT VS. FORCE

Attempting to force goodness by yelling or lecturing communicates to teenagers that we consider their behavior *our* responsibility rather than *theirs*. It strips them of ownership for their goodness or badness. It prevents them from carving out their own moral decisions, and ultimately sustains a state of moral immaturity.

All of us would agree that we want our teens to take responsibility for themselves. We want them to clean up after themselves, to act decently, to get to school on time, and so forth. While our tendency may be to bail teenagers out when they fail, nothing could be worse in many cases. It isn't until they shoulder the weight of irresponsibility that responsibility will look more appealing. It isn't until they have, in one sense or another paid for, cried over, and mended the results of their wrongs, that alternative behaviors make sense.

One father I spoke with recently had caught his seventeen-year-old squealing the tires on the family's car. When he confronted the boy about it, they agreed that another infraction of that type would result in the son buying two new rear tires for the car. "It's a shame though," this father shared with me. "I know William and he knows me. I know he'll never spin those tires again . . . and I really could use some new rear tires!" Both William and his dad have learned that logical consequences are invaluable. Nothing is as effective as placing the responsibility right in one's lap.

If it is a child's responsibility to do the dishes and he doesn't, then we may need to leave the dirty dishes piled high in the sink. Then wake him up a half-hour earlier the next morning to wash them—after all the food has dried on. The labor that results from his procrastination will motivate him more than a lecture would have the night before.

The key is to think ahead and plan for logical consequences that will teach, as opposed to yelling or using guilt trips to coerce behavior. How would you modify a teen's habit of leaving the lights on much of the time? One family I spoke with just deducted fifty cents from the child's weekly allowance for each infraction, to help with the electric bill. They said it took about two months and then the problem subsided to a very tolerable level. At that point they discarded the allowance deduction, stating that they would reinstate it again if needed.

How would you teach the logical consequence of getting in after a stated curfew? One set of parents I know set up a system whereby if a curfew was exceeded, they would change the curfew for the next month to be that much (the amount of the excess) earlier. For example, if a teen is twenty minutes late, then he or she needs to be in twenty minutes earlier than normal for a month. After the month is up the record is clear, and the original curfew time is reinstated. With a little forethought, the possibilities are amazing.

As teenagers grow into late adolescence it becomes imperative that adults allow the great teacher called "consequences" to teach responsible behavior. John White, having lived with the heartbreak of a son who chose to oppose his parents' faith, writes about the need for letting go of responsibility for poor choices as late adolescence emerges:

> Parents who cling to their erring children must realize that by paying debts and legal expenses . . . or even by offering continued shelter, food, and clothing, they can morally become a party to the delinquent behavior. Their actions can make it possible for rebellious children to continue to live as they have in the past. Home for them is merely a free hotel. Instead of helping them to follow godliness, parents are giving their children the message that there is no need for them to be godly, since their parents will always look after them and get them out of a hole.[7]

The Norman-Harris Report asked teenagers what would prevent teens from shoplifting. Their number one answer? Getting caught![8] Teenagers come to genuinely regard the need for moral behavior when they've experienced the consequences of the opposite.

I have come up with an acrostic that helps me remember what it takes for teens to make better choices on their own. Belief, Expectation, Trial, Time, Encouragement, and Realization (B-E-T-T-E-R). In helping teenagers improve their moral batting average, I apply this acrostic almost daily. It begins with my clearly affirming their potential. They need to know I believe the best of them and will continue to, even in the face of failure.

Second, I attempt to explain exactly what is expected of them and why, giving them a strong rationale for change. Third, I help them define a challenge or temptation—something that will test their ability to act appropriately—and help them to determine exactly what will define success or failure. It needs to be clear. Fourth, we give it some time. I communicate that I don't expect overnight change from them any more than

I expect it from myself. I let them know that real behavior change requires a tough and sometimes lengthy process. Teens need to know that. Many of them lose hope because they feel as though they're supposed to have it all together yesterday. In fact, knowing that is an important part of the next step, encouragement. Teenagers, as well as adults, thrive on it. Performance escalates when encouragement is genuine.

The final factor is realization. So often, we don't do enough reveling in our successes. Think about it. Don't we tend to focus on what hasn't been done, the problems that still exist, the sins we still battle? Yet nothing inspires holiness more than celebrating the conquest of our enemies. What you do to celebrate is up to you and it will change depending on the issue involved, but whatever you do—stop and enjoy even the smallest advancements in the right direction.

While there are no guarantees, there is hope. Teenagers are changing, and they're changing faster than they will at any other time of life. In just a few years they'll go from being completely childlike to being a functioning adult. The transition isn't a clean break by any means but it is happening, setbacks and all. God is using your love, example, forgiveness, and patience to create a life that brings Him glory.

NOTES:

1. Lawrence Kohlberg and Carol Gilligan, "The Adolescent as a Philosopher," from Jerome Kagan and Robert Coles, eds., *Twelve—Sixteen Early Adolescence* (New York: W.W. Norton, 1972), pp. 165-68.

2. Earl D. Wilson, *Try Being a Teenager* (Portland: Multnomah Press, 1982), p. 123.

3. Robert Laurent, *Keeping Your Teen in Touch with God* (Elgin, Illinois: David C. Cook Publishing Co., 1988), p. 96.

4. Dr. James Dobson, *Dare to Discipline* (Wheaton: Tyndale, 1970), p. 36.

5. Dr. Bruce Narramore, *Help I'm a Parent* (Grand Rapids: Zondervan, 1972), p. 41.

6. Daniel O. Aleshire, *Understanding Today's Youth* (Nashville: Convention Press, 1982), pp. 67-8.

7. John White, *Parents in Pain* (Downers Grove: Intervarsity Press, 1979), p. 204.

8. Jane Norman and Myron Harris, *The Private Life of the American Teenager* (New York: Rawson, Wade Publishers, Inc., 1981), p. 261.

SPREADING THEIR WINGS FOR FLIGHT

At the Right Time, Step Back, Trust God, and Let Them Go

The challenge of granting autonomy can be excruciating. As teens mature, we're tempted to do almost anything to help them avoid costly mistakes. Yet by allowing a teenager to exercise his own decision-making muscles, we set up a process by which the values we've instilled over the years can be carried right on into adulthood.

It was an older home with grass growing through cracks in the sidewalk and overgrown shrubs looming over the lawn. Gary escorted me inside. The smell of antiseptic hit me as my eyes adjusted to the dim living room light. "These are my patients," Gary informed me as weary, aged people greeted me warmly.

Sandra, Gary's mom, poked her head out through the kitchen doorway. "This is it," she said, smiling. "This is Gary's domain."

Another woman walked through the room and offered a drink of juice to a man propped up with pillows in a wheel chair. "Gary, would you get Mrs. Jenners a blanket for her lap?" Gary left the room.

"Are you working here too?" I asked Sandra.

"No, I just came by to say 'hi' to Gary." She stepped closer and lowered her voice. "Daniel, Gary is doing really well. He completed four classes this semester at Highline Community College, and he's really anxious to get started on his major."

"His major?" I asked. "He knows what he wants to study?"

"Yes, didn't he tell you? He wants to be a social worker. He's also thinking about hospital administration. They have a good program for that at the college.

"He's attending a college group at another church now, too. Can you believe it? I wish he'd go to church with us, but we know he just needs to make a clean break. He didn't want people remembering his past every time he shows up."

"I can understand that," I conceded.

"I never thought it would be this hard—letting him go. He's had so many problems . . . but now all we can do is hang on to the Lord. We just hope Gary hangs on to Him too."

Like Gary's parents, we're constantly in the process of releasing. From the moment of birth, children are gaining independence. Even in childhood they're acquiring skills that will allow them to function successfully as an autonomous adult. That, in fact, is the goal of good parenting. It's the goal of good youth guidance in any form. But the breaking away is painful. Molding another life is like painstakingly weaving a tapestry. So much of one's self has been invested in the process. A person doesn't part with it easily.

"I just shudder to think of all that is out there," Karen's mom confided one day. "Karen gets so dependent on people—especially guys, if she thinks they like her. I just want her to make it on her own, but I'm so scared she's going to do something really dumb. Things are just so different than when I left home."

Granted, things are different. They always are. But the challenge of letting go and trusting God to watch over and work out the lives of those we love, isn't a new one. The questions are the same for every generation: How much do we let out the reigns? How soon? On which issues? How do we let go gradually as our teens gets older? How do we keep the leash from snapping, only to lose them in a torrent of rebellion? How do we relax, with full knowledge of the pitfalls and passions that exist in a world we can't control?

Let's dip one more time into the pages of the past. What we'll discover is that God identifies with our dilemma. In fact, He's prepared to protect those we prize.

Oppression in the Israelite camps had reached an intolerable high. The Pharaoh was becoming more impatient with his work projects at Pithom and Ramses, and that impatience was being taken out on the slave labor he exacted from the Israelite people. As months passed, his anger mingled with fear, resulting in a decree that all Israelite baby boys must be slaughtered at birth. Panic erupted among God's people!

Jochabed knew the decree, she knew her own death could result from disobedience of it, she knew God could protect her if He wished to. She also knew she was pregnant.

Miriam, Jochabed's daughter, did what she could to comfort her mother through the long hours of delivery but finally the announcement came: Jochabed had given birth to a son. Months went by and Jochabed did what she could to hide her baby, but it became apparent that her secret was going to be discovered sooner or later.

As the morning sky first showed signs of light, Jochabed slipped away from her tent and walked silently to the bank of the Nile. Her baby cradled in one arm, she carried a papyrus basket in the other. Sneaking through the reeds, she found a place where the water was quiet — a place where members of the royal family often came to bathe in the morning. Wrapping her son in a soft wool blanket, she placed him in the basket which she had lovingly crafted out of reeds and pitch. She bent close and kissed her baby on the cheek.

Miriam had followed Jochabed at a distance and now waited amid thick brush to see what would happen. Jochabed turned and headed back for camp, while Miriam remained hidden by the foliage. Cradled in his floating basket, the gentle movement of the water lulled the child to sleep. Miriam, knowing that women from the palace would soon be arriving, just waited and watched.

As expected, Pharaoh's daughter, followed by an entourage of attendants, came walking along the river's bank. They made their way into the alcove where Jochabed's baby was floating in his bassinet boat. The voices and laughter startled him and he began to cry. Pharaoh's daughter stopped. She moved through the reeds, following the sound of the baby's cries, and found the basket where Jochabed had left it.

"Look," she exclaimed to her aides, "it's a baby!" She picked the boy up from his basket and cradled him in her arms. "Someone has abandoned him here. He's a Hebrew," she said, looking into his frightened brown eyes. Miriam emerged from the brush as casually as possible.

"Good morning," Miriam offered. "I didn't know you had a baby!" The princess looked bewildered.

"Well, I don't. Actually, I just found him here among the reeds."

Miriam bent close to look at her brother, as if she'd never seen him before. "He looks like an Israelite baby to me," she whispered. "Would you like me to go into the Israelite camp to see if I can find someone to care for him?"

"Yes! Go right away," Pharaoh's daughter commanded. "Find someone who can nurse him. I'll stay here until you return."

Miriam ran to Jochabed's tent and told her the news. Within minutes the two of them arrived back at the river. The princess explained to Jochabed how she had found the child. Then she said, "Take care of him for me and I will pay you well to protect him from my father. He is beautiful. I don't want anything to happen to him. Once he's grown to be a small boy I will raise him in the palace."

Jochabed could feel her heart pounding as she listened intently. She took the baby in her arms and promised the princess her devotion to the child for as long as the princess desired.

Jochabed raised her child, teaching him about the Hebrew God even from infancy. One day, just as the princess had said, she visited Jochabed, paid her a hefty sum of money for her nurturing, and took the child to live in the royal palace. "I will call him Moses," she explained, which in Egyptian means "to draw out" or "to be born." "I will call him Moses because I drew him out of the Nile River and saved his life."

But the true story of Moses and his miraculous deliverance spread throughout the Israelite camp. A Hebrew child in the palace! What would his destiny be? All Jochabed could do was trust God to see Moses through the hurdles that lay before him as a prince in one of the most powerful and godless kingdoms on earth (Exodus 2).

Jochabed's experience is like ours. We hand God our kids. We cover our eyes. "OK, God, you can have them. We can't hang on to them forever. But God, please take care of them. Do you really love them as much as we do?"

It can feel like you're putting a loaded gun into your child's hand sometimes. Can he really handle life by himself without getting hurt? After all, you've been there for so long. If you're his parent, your input has been the lifeblood of that kid. You've guarded him from infancy. You changed all those diapers. You taught him to talk. You held him after he went down on his bike and got all scraped up. You bought him a Bible. You showed him the world. You gave him manners and skills and confidence. You told him to do things for himself. You taught him to think on his own. And now—he's doing it. There's pride in that. And pain.

Adults have a great responsibility to their teenagers: they must let them go. We are to be there for support, for ideas, and for guidance, but should not hold teens down as tightly as we needed to when they were younger. While this isn't easy, or even a "clean job," there are qualities of character that will get us through. There are gifts we can give them, even in the turmoil of emancipation. These are the great gifts that echo in their memory long after they're on their own.

Respect their personhood despite change.

Older teens are changing fast. Obviously. And they're aware that they're changing. They see themselves acting more responsibly at times. They're experiencing new depths to their emotions. They see themselves becoming more skilled.

At the same time, they're acutely aware of their shortcomings. They are comparing themselves with adults and adult characteristics. They're sensing that their efforts are constantly colliding with their potential and it frustrates them to no end.

I greatly appreciate an illustration Bruce Narramore uses:

> Because separating from you and tackling adulthood isn't easy, most adolescents rock back and forth between developmental stages a bit like a car stuck in the mud. When you first push it forward, you go only an inch or two. Then you let it rock back and gain momentum for a harder shove. After several efforts back and forth, it rocks far back—almost as though you are losing ground—but this provides the final momentum to push it over the hump. Your teenagers' occasionally childish times actually help them get ready to move ahead. Then, once they clear a developmental hurdle, they gain additional momentum and experience a strengthening of their personalities that ushers in a period of increased stability or calm.[1]

Because this vacillation between childhood and adulthood is so apparent, the very real question of "Who am I" keeps rearing up before them. They may come to doubt their value as a person. They worry over what they are or aren't becoming.

RANDY DISPLAYED EXCEPTIONAL MATURITY throughout high school, and got along pretty well with both his parents and his peers. He graduated. He started classes at a Bible college nearby. Randy had been given various responsibilities within our youth group, he held a job at a local department store and maintained decent grades without too much effort. But things slowly began to deteriorate. He started showing up late. Commitments were being dropped. He appeared somewhat apathetic about failures brought to his attention.

One December morning, Jean came to my office. "Daniel, Dennis and I really support Randy now that he's started college, but he's impossible to live with. He's always been a really responsible kid, but now it seems like he's regressing. He comes home late. He forgets to do the chores we've given him around the house. In fact, his employer called me just the other day and wondered what was wrong with him.

Just after the first of the year, I had the opportunity to sit down with Randy. At first he acted as though everything was fine. Finally, I said, "Randy, let me take a guess at how you might be feeling these days. You know you've got a lot going for you. You've got some great friends. You're doing well in school. You work hard at getting along with your parents. You're an excellent leader here in our youth group. But . . . " I paused. Randy looked at me as if I were about to tell him his fortune.

" . . . You're tired of being responsible. You want some slack. You just want to be free to do what you want for a change. And you're doing some of that, but it bothers you because you know you're letting people down. You're feeling caught in the middle." Randy stared right at me.

"That's exactly how I feel," he replied slowly.

The two of us spent the next hour talking about the future. Randy was feeling floored by the pressures of adulthood. They seemed overwhelming. So we talked about pressure and the freedoms that accompany responsibility. We talked about how to distinguish between times to "cut loose" and times to "come through."

Randy's perspective began a slow change for the better. By spring he seemed to exude a maturity that I'd never seen before. His lapse backward into more adolescent behaviors seemed to provide something of a reprieve, and with time he had accumulated the personal reserves necessary to move forward.

During this back and forth period, teenagers are desperately looking to adults for affirmation. They're dying to know that they are lovable, loved, and wonderful in the present. In the midst of growing from dependent childhood toward independent adulthood, teenagers are relying on adults to believe in them, even while they are very much in process.

Respecting a teenager's personhood is communicated in a variety of ways: Giving them ample time to express their ideas and ideals. Encouraging them to evaluate personal characteristics apart from our input. And expressing our belief in their abilities, interests, and in their potential as emerging adults.

One of the great joys in my ministry comes from helping teenagers who have been content to coast along as idle observers switch into gear and become motivated leaders. I'm often aware that teenagers feel caught by the past. They know they're capable of becoming more mature but they're afraid of the change.

Helping them move forward requires a great deal of belief in their capacity to operate as mature, effective adults, even in complex situations. Attempting never to minimize the importance of even their smallest advances, my goal is to show them that they can and will be successful as individuals.

Respect their choices despite their immaturity.

Choice-making is a new art for adolescents. Even kids who have been given the opportunity to make choices while growing up are faced with all sorts of wonderful, and sometimes dangerous, options. The freedom to choose is a freedom we value most as humans. Adolescence is a time of breaking into that big new world.

Choices are everywhere. *Now that I have options, which class should I take? Now that I have a license, where should I go? And how fast should I go? Which girl should I date? Which personality traits should I emulate? Which activities should I pursue? How far can I go and survive? How daring can I be?* So much adventure!

Adults, on the other hand, are attempting to protect. They're trying to channel the exuberance. They're aware of the dangers. They're aware that too much freedom too soon can be disastrous:

> When children are in adolescence, their parents usually enter middle age. The combination of these two life stages complicates the generation gap. While young people experiment with new behaviors, stretch

their limits and take risks, their parents become more conservative. While youth experience exuberance and idealism, parents realistically evaluate the status of their finances and health for their later years. Young people see no end to life and instinctively rebel against its boundaries. But their middle-aged parents see friends and relatives dying, recognize a feeling of "It's too late," and learn to respect life's cautions and limitations. Is it any surprise there is conflict as the energy of adolescence collides with the realism of middle age?[2]

Recently, Jimmy volunteered to drive for one of our weekend retreats in the mountains. He had told a number of students that he was driving and offered to take them. Friday morning arrived and Jimmy called me.

"My parents won't let me drive," Jimmy explained with a note of exasperation in his voice. "They say it's too far and they're worried about the curvy mountain roads. I don't see why they're so uptight. I'm a really good driver. What am I going to tell all those kids who wanted to go with me?"

"I think they'll understand. Don't sweat it, Jimmy." But he sweated it anyway. To Jimmy, the issue was monumental.

I pulled into the parking lot at church and was surprised to find Jimmy standing there next to his dad's truck. "We went and bought chains," he said with a smile. "I get to drive."

While wise protection is necessary, overprotection is a common problem and can be nearly as destructive as indifference. Overprotection becomes apparent when adults have a hard time trusting teens to think on their own, to make decisions, and to handle many of life's circumstances on their own. It's one thing to listen, ask questions, and to be available for help at the teenager's request. Involvement is helpful. But it's another thing, and an unfortunate one, when adults offer a dump-truck load of advice, spew out solutions, and take over decision-making, either emotionally or actually. That's overprotection.

One result of overprotection is moral retardation. Without the harsh realities of life, a teenager has nothing upon which to

One result of overprotection is moral retardation. Without the harsh realities of life, a teenager has nothing upon which to cut the teeth of true character. It takes abrasion to sharpen metal, or a mind for that matter. Overprotection can breed conformity and comfort. In the short run, its appeal is great. However, with time, conformity easily transforms itself into dishonesty, and comfort can deteriorate into apathy.

> **Children reared in warm but restrictive (as opposed to autonomy-encouraging) homes are likely to be dependent and conforming; less aggressive, dominant and competitive with peers; less friendly; less creative; and more hostile in their fantasies. In contrast, those reared in homes where parental love is evident though not cloying, and where the child is given considerable age-appropriate autonomy, are likely to emerge as more active, outgoing, socially assertive, and independent, as well as friendly, creative, and lacking in hostility toward others or self. While such children may also tend to be somewhat disobedient, disrespectful, and rebellious on occasion, these behaviors appear to manifest themselves largely because of feelings of security and lack of severe punitive response from parents . . . .[3]**

I've heard parents tell me all about how wonderful their little Susie was until she went to that new school, got involved in a new youth group, went off to the Navy . . . whatever. They point a critical finger at some institution or person, but never at their own child.

Chances are, some circumstance provoked a new-found sense of freedom from mom and dad, and the adolescent inside was released on the world. The restrictions were lowered, the props were removed, the choices were no longer being forced. Consequently, the kid decided to explore his freedom and make some decisions of his own for once. Ideally, the reins could have been loosened earlier, a little at a time, and the flight for freedom may have been less explosive.

Watching a young person play the field of real-life experiences is scary viewing! Yet the fact remains: Unless we cut some slack, the leash will break and destructive behaviors may intensify. Adults must honor this search for personal convictions. We must allow teenagers to make choices, even poor ones, in order to work their decision-making muscles. When the furnace of trial and error has refined behavior, then good choices will indeed be "owned" and will be acted upon in the future.

Karen's parents faced a common problem during her senior year. They had co-signed the papers for the loan on Karen's new Honda. They had done so with the understanding that she would make the payments, no matter what. But as time went on they found themselves making part of the payments for her. She still had a job but there was always something—new clothes or a concert or new ski boots—that prevented her from having enough money for the next payment.

"Should we help her out with the payments so she can keep the car or what?" Darlene had asked.

I proceeded to ask Darlene a few questions as well. By the end of our conversation she had concluded that even if Karen lost the car, she needed to develop responsibility for herself. At this point, Darlene concluded, Karen needed the character more than the car. She gave Karen one last notice and helped her through the current month. The next month rolled around. Karen came up short. Darlene stuck by her guns. Karen ended up being late on her payments—and scared to death. Rather, she was scared into *life*, life in the real world, you might say. To my knowledge, she's made every payment since.

Consider the findings of research in this area:

Many adults do not shoulder responsibility because during their youth, well-meaning parents and friends bailed them out every time they failed to follow through with responsibilities. They were never allowed to learn from their mistakes.

It appears that the carrying of responsibility for oneself and others contributes to moral development.

Those who reach the highest levels of moral development are those who have had responsibility for their own lives and the lives of others.[4]

My own parents were well aware of my shortcomings as an adolescent. They knew that no great ballplayer hits a home run every time. They let me make mistakes and suffer the consequences. When I stole, I took it back *and* paid for it. When I had problems with other students, they generally asked how I planned on working it out. When I failed to come through on a responsibility, my freedom was restricted until I accomplished all that I was expected to do. They rarely prevented me from blundering, refused to make excuses for me, and never bailed me out. At the time I didn't appreciate it at all. Today, I consider them heroes.

Respect their faith despite their doubts.

Nothing is harder for Christian parents than to watch adolescents question their faith. As a pastor to young people, nothing bewilders me more than wondering if anything "spiritual" is taking shape.

Children who are raised in a Christian home environment encounter a problem that other children don't have. They must somehow move from an acceptance of their parents' faith to a point where they embrace a faith of their own. It's tough enough for them to internalize personally what has been such a constant since the day they were born. But when a kid's parents don't realize how important it is to allow him to make up his own mind, the problem is compounded.

When a teenager is so coerced into adopting his parents' position on issues of faith that he has no space to develop his own convictions, a sense of false security is inevitable. He may think he's going to heaven just because his parents are. He may feel totally ambivalent about making a commitment to Christ personally. Down the road, he may sense the void in his own life and become dissatisfied with the idea of faith altogether. After all, it's not working for him personally. In actuality, he's never owned it himself.

Values assumed without question usually wear thin when the pressure of compromise is on and no one is watching. Like attempting to force a big balloon into a small jar, when convictions are forced, the result is that rebellion will pop out wherever there is an opening. Adults who can allow teens to express the ups and downs of internalizing values will see less reactionary rebellion than adults who become stifling and defensive during the process.

So what can we do when doubts begin to chop away at a teenager's faith? First, we must realize that doubts are actually construction blocks that we use to solidify what we believe. In order to be convinced of anything, we must evaluate the options. Kids who never have doubts may not really be thinking through the issues involved.

Second, we need to relax and provide an open forum for the discussion of doubts. While holding firmly to our own perspectives and defending how we have arrived at our conclusions, we can be equally as interested in their opposing viewpoints. Teenagers are primarily concerned about having a place to share. They need someone who understands. Our agreeing with them isn't nearly as important.

Third, in every way possible we need to give them responsibility for the development of their own faith. Have them lead in prayer. Ask them what they think about a moral issue that comes up. Find out how they would solve an ethical dilemma. Encourage them to share what they're learning and feeling as they move through their personal spiritual journey. That sense of your respect for their faith, even as it is being formed, will help to cement belief long after you're through driving them to Sunday school.

"I BELIEVE MY PARENTS respect me more now." The wind whipped a scattering of November leaves around the playground. Karen looked thoughtfully across the field that was the battleground for the Mason High Bobcats. "I'm applying to go to college back East next fall. My dad doesn't want me to go that far from home. Besides, it's not a Christian college or anything. I think he's afraid I'm going to crash and burn."

"What do you think, Karen?" I asked.

"I think I can handle it. You know, ever since I went to Mexico and saw how the rest of the world lives . . . I don't know. It's like I feel freer now. I feel like it's not just my parent's faith anymore. It's more my own, you know?"

"I do," I said. "I know exactly what you mean."

Karen has done just that. She lives on the East coast now. She's dating a Christian guy and is plugged in to an on-campus fellowship of believers. Karen's life as a committed disciple has taken flight.

Respect their need to be trusted despite their setbacks.

What are teenagers' most deeply felt needs? In most cases they want to feel trusted and respected, even while they are fumbling. Teenagers desperately want, and need, the trust of adults, even as they misuse it. Despite their inability to always be trustworthy with the freedoms they are granted, to stop trusting is to communicate that they can't handle responsibility. Once the kid himself believes that, he's doomed to repeat cycles of ineptitude.

I asked more than one hundred teenagers, "What comments or suggestions would you make to your parents, if you could be completely honest?" Many of their responses had to do with trust. According to the comments I received, most teens don't feel like they have "arrived," or are always handling freedom perfectly. Yet in order to grow into adults, they're crying out to be trusted and given room to try, even if that trying results in some setbacks. Listen in on some of what they said:

"Can't you trust kids to have their own judgment?"

"I think you know I don't do any awful things, such as drugs, or drinking, so please don't ground me so hard when I come home fifteen minutes late."

"Let me be myself! I'm not perfect like you!"

"You say it's not that you don't trust me, it's that you don't trust the people I'm with. But, if you really trusted me, you would trust me to pick the right kind of friends."

"Don't try to step in and solve all my problems for me. Trust me. I can figure things out better on my own."

"Why do you always demand to know everything that is not your business?"

"Why won't you believe me?"

Over and over, students simply stated in a variety of ways, *Please trust me more.*

Feelings of mistrust are a major factor in family disunity. Teens who sense mistrust will eventually conclude that they simply are not trustworthy. It's the "If that's the way they think I am, that's what I will be" syndrome, and that is stifling to ethical growth.

It is extremely difficult to rise above the expectations of the people around us. Teens feel that more acutely than anyone. If we can acknowledge failure and then get right back to trusting, adolescents feel the freedom to behave more appropriately in the future. Nothing is more suffocating than the feeling that we've disobeyed to the point of no return. It's true that God calls sin "sin," but He never fails to trust us with another try at righteousness. Never.

As teenagers get older, one important way that trust is communicated is through our respect of their privacy. I appreciate the perspective of Earl Wilson on this important point:

> Trust is more important than information in most cases. I find that I get information whether I want it or not. I usually don't accomplish anything by invading my teenager's privacy. Being available is more effective in gathering information than spying or playing Twenty Questions. It is difficult for parents not to worry about their teenagers because parents know most of the potential problem areas that teenagers face. However, invasion of privacy will not allay your worries. In fact, invasion of privacy will probably make your worries worse.[5]

I would bet that every month I encounter at least one adult who has discovered something disappointing about the teen he or she is close to. They find a note in the pocket of the pants they are about to wash, or take a phone message from a guy that is bad news to be hanging around with, or discover a pornographic magazine under the mattress.

Those revelations are inevitable and can provide a springboard for discussion. However, great harm is done when we begin rifling through belongings or make inquiries of friends in order to dig up clues to misbehavior. Once that is detected by the adolescent, they've got equal grounds for mistrusting us! We're no longer "playing fair."

Respect their attempts despite their failure.

Where there is attempted responsibility, there is partial success at best, and utter failure at the worst. In either case, encouragement will keep the machinery of independence chugging and sputtering along. I know of no other factor in the equation of encouragement that is more important than forgiveness. Brush strokes of forgiveness paint a world of encouragement. Forgiveness gives teenagers the guts to continue, even after multiple defeats.

During my own rebellious teenage years there was a woman who always took me back, no matter how badly I acted. Eve Olson. She was a middle-aged woman who lived on a farm way out in the country near the little chalk-white church I attended.

Whether it was the church Christmas play that was not turning out, or a broken relationship with a girlfriend, or feelings of doubt about the existence of God, Eve was there offering encouragement.

As far as I can remember, she never belittled my tiny advancements toward spiritual maturity or moral goodness. When I visited rest homes with the youth group, she pointed out the tremendous value of the effort. When I told the truth, even in the face of personal loss, she noticed. When I helped clean up trash after a church picnic, she gave ample attention to the deed. She realized my successes with me. She made a bigger deal of those than she did my failures. We celebrated my accomplishments with gusto.

It seemed like she always treated my blunders and sins as if they were exceptions to the rule. Often I would overhear her tell some other adult what a terrific kid I was. Never once can I remember her telling others of my failures. No matter how dark things got, or how much pain I caused, I knew she believed in me and remained on my side. This freed me up to pursue my best.

To this day Eve lives on in my memory as a heroine simply because she didn't throw in the towel, or, worse yet, strangle me with it. I can still hear her cheering from the back row when our miserable bathrobe Christmas play ended. She'd meet us backstage with hugs and kisses and tell us that God was going to do great things through each and every one of us. And you know, after all these years, I still believe He will.

Nothing is as powerful as expectation. When we expect failure, it usually follows. When we expect success, our chances of seeing success are multiplied greatly.

My parents did an amazing thing when I was sixteen years old. They not only allowed me to go to Europe as an exchange student, but they let me travel throughout the continent with two other teenagers for a month—unsupervised! Too reckless for your blood? Maybe so.

From the moment we began discussing the trip, I knew exactly what their expectations were of me. They believed in my ability to make wise decisions, and they expected nothing less. There were no lectures and no stern warnings. They communicated over and over how well they knew I would do on my own. When asked, they offered valuable advice. That was all.

Mom and Dad expected one other thing above all else: They firmly expected God to watch over me. They always made it clear that they were praying for me daily. They had entrusted me to God and relied on Him to supervise my life when I was beyond their grasp. That left a deep impression on me. The power of their expectation lifted me beyond countless hurdles. That trip to Europe was one of the greatest experiences of my life.

Every now and then I encounter a student who feels that, no matter what he does right, his parents won't be satisfied. When that truly is the case, it's a tragedy. Nothing inspires independent righteousness more than an inner sense of accomplishment. When you see that you *can* be good, you *want* to be good. Realizing that you're succeeding creates a greater excitement for doing well. It works on the snowball effect.

UNCLIPPING THE LEASH

Not long ago I was taking a stroll near our home and I noticed a middle-aged man walking his large black Lab just ahead of me. In one hand he held the dog's leash. In the other hand he had a Frisbee. The dog's exuberance over the very thought of chasing the Frisbee could hardly be contained.

As they neared an intersection, I noticed that the man kept the dog close to his side. They passed a baby nuzzled down in his stroller, which attracted the dog's interest. The man held the leash tight and kept the dog out of trouble. As they walked along, the dog kept leaping ahead of his master, nipping at the Frisbee. With some irritation, the man would swat at the dog, which calmed things only momentarily.

At one point the owner acted as though he were getting ready to throw the Frisbee. The dog naturally came unglued with anticipation. It lunged forward and was jerked back by the leash on its neck.

The little game continued for a while as we all walked on. Finally, the two of them arrived at a large grassy area. While the man bent down and unclipped the leash, the dog went berserk with joy. At long last the Frisbee was released into the air with a whoosh over the Lab's head, and grass went flying as the dog peeled out after it. Across the lawn the dog grabbed the Frisbee between his teeth and pranced back to his master for another round.

I was struck by the parallels between this and the long process of releasing teens. Tension increases as teenagers become more adept at life. They know more. They're more self-sufficient. They can get around without a lot of supervision. They feel their potential. But they also feel the constraints holding them back. Curfews. Standards. Responsibilities. Limited skills. Expectations. The leash feels tight.

There will be times when adults must hold on tightly. But as time progresses, the leash will become a noose if it is not loosened. Teenagers must be free to run ahead, play the field, explore the turf. There are risks involved, but life is like that.

When teenagers are given room to expand their wings, amazing things can happen. Remember David? Scholars tell us he was a just a young kid when he killed Goliath and saved the army of Israel. God believed in David and took him out of the sheepfold to shepherd His people. And Josiah? It was during his teenage years that he brought about the most radical spiritual reforms Israel had ever known. And there was Daniel, who was taken into Babylonian captivity while probably just a young man. He fared far better than the rest of Israel when asked to stand for his faith in God. And Mary was just a teenager when she was entrusted with nurturing God's own Son.

And my friends that you've met? What has become of them? All of them have launched into life. Gary is caring for his gang of senior citizens and attends an excellent college group at another church. Karen is on the East Coast, working with a campus fellowship. She wrote recently of her plans to marry a guy she's been seeing for the past year. Sarah ended up leaving the "scummy cafe" after all. She's attending a trade college to develop secretarial skills, shares an apartment with a couple of girlfriends, and is continuing to grow through personal counseling, as well as through a support group she attends. But the best part is—she's dating Randy! The two of them show up together on Saturday nights for our contemporary worship service and Randy continues to work with his own small group of guys while going to college. It's a struggle, but all of them are cutting their spiritual teeth on real life-on-life discipleship.

Jimmy is in his second year of Bible college and is giving serious consideration to becoming, of all things, a youth pastor.

"Are you crazy?" I joked. Jimmy had just changed his major from business to youth ministry and called to tell me about it. "Yeah, I guess I am. That's why I think I'd do well working with teenagers."

BUILDING A MONUMENT THAT BREATHES

One drizzly gray June morning a few years ago, I stood like an ant in front of an enormous structure in the heart of London. I entered St. Paul's Cathedral and began my routine of reading brochures and guide books, and eavesdropping on English-speaking guides that led small groups of tourists through a myriad of corridors. The longer I observed and listened, the more impressed I became, not with the structure itself, but with the visionary who had built it.

Sir Christopher Wren, I learned, had never been trained as an architect. He had studied math and astronomy but never architecture. He had a lot of other projects going on at the same time. In fact, he had fifty other buildings in process during the same period of time in which he was at work on this one. Gothic was in vogue, but he personally preferred other forms. So, he went against the grain and built what he envisioned, while critics scoffed. There were countless setbacks and delays. The process of building took much longer, was much more difficult, and cost much more than planned.

Descending worn stone steps, I entered into the crypt below the church to view the tombs of the fathers and artisans buried there. Many were ornately carved. Some were massive. But the one that caught my attention was simple; in fact, it was notably plain. This was the grave of Sir Christopher Wren. I can't any longer remember it exactly but the inscription on the front read something like this: "You Look To Find My Monument? Simply Look Around You."

Up on the main floor again I sat down on a quiet bench beneath the 365-foot-high dome that caps the structure. I thought about the effort required to build, not structures, but people. So often the journey is marked by a similar set of circumstances. There really isn't any training for what we encounter with an adolescent, other than what we learn in the school called "Experience." *We are unprepared.*

And, isn't it true that the process of building a life could well consume all of our time and emotional energy? Yet all the while, reality dishes out a host of other concerns and responsibilities. *We are stretched thin.*

When was the last time a teenager sat you down to praise your work and admire your sacrifice? *We are rarely appreciated.*

Isn't it amazing how long it takes to help another emerging adult get his or her act together? *We are anxious.*

And have you noticed there are no parties thrown for people who gut it out in the trench of parental duty or Christian discipleship? No ticker tape floats down from heaven. There are no banners along the hard-won path. *We are unheralded.*

But there is a monument that breathes. There is a person who has forever been shaped by our devotion, despite the disappointments. There is a life that will exist long after cathedrals crumble. Our task is to prepare this child well for that eternal journey, then to let go of him. To watch him wabble for a time—and then begin to fly.

NOTES:

1. Bruce Narramore, *Cutting the Cord* (Wheaton: Tyndale, 1990), p. 36.

2. G. Keith Olson, *Why Teenagers Act the Way They Do* (Loveland: Group, 1987), p. 32.

3. John Conger, "A World They Never Knew," from Jerome Kagan and Robert Coles, eds., *Twelve—Sixteen Early Adolescence* (New York: W.W. Norton, 1972), p. 215.

4. Catherine M. Stonehouse, *Patterns in Moral Development* (Waco: Word, 1980), p. 70.

5. Earl D. Wilson, *Try Being a Teenager* (Portland: Multnomah Press, 1982), p. 62.

BIBLIOGRAPHY

BOOKS

Alcorn, Randy C. *Christians in the Wake of the Sexual Revolution*. Portland: Multnomah Press, 1985.

Aleshire, Daniel O. *Understanding Today's Youth*. Nashville: Convention Press, 1982.

Borthwick, Paul. *But You Don't Understand*. Nashville: Oliver Nelson, 1982.

Campbell, Ross, M.D. *How to Really Love Your Teenager*. Wheaton: Scripture Press, 1977.

Campbell, Ross, M.D. *Kids Who Follow, Kids Who Don't*. Wheaton: Scripture Press, 1987.

Campolo, Anthony. *Growing Up in America*. Grand Rapids: Zondervan, 1989.

Coles, Robert. *The Moral Life of Children*. Boston: Atlantic Monthly Press, 1986.

Conger, John. *Adolescence: Generation Under Pressure*. New York: Harper and Row, 1979.

Clouse, Bonnidell. *Moral Development: Perspectives in Psychology and Christian Belief*. Grand Rapids: Baker, 1985.

de Vinck, Christopher. *Power of the Powerless*. New York: Doubleday, 1988.

Dobson, James. *Dare to Discipline*. Wheaton: Tyndale, 1970.

Dobson, James. *Parenting Isn't for Cowards*. Waco: Word, 1987.

Elkind, David. *All Grown Up and No Place to Go*. Reading, Massachusetts: Addison-Wesley Publishing Company, 1984.

Hunt, Gary and Angela. *Surviving the Tweenage Years: A Guide for Parents and Youth Workers*. San Bernardino: Here's Life Publishers, 1988.

Kagan, Jerome and Robert Coles, eds. *Twelve—Sixteen Early Adolescence*. New York: W.W. Norton, 1972.

Kesler, Jay. *Ten Mistakes Parents Make with Teenagers: And How to Avoid Them*. Brentwood, Tennessee: Wolgemuth and Hyatt Publishers, 1988.

Kimmel, Tim. *Legacy of Love: A Plan for Parenting on Purpose*. Portland: Multnomah Press, 1989.

Koteskey, Ronald L. *Understanding Adolescence*. Wheaton: Scripture Press Publications, 1987.

Laurent, Robert. *Keeping Your Teen in Touch with God*. Elgin, Illinois: David C. Cook Publishing Co, 1988.

Leman, Kevin. *Smart Kids, Stupid Choices*. Ventura: Gospel Light Publications, 1982.

Mc Dowell, Josh. *What I Wish My Parents Knew about My Sexuality*. San Bernardino: Here's Life Publishers, 1987.

Mc Dowell, Josh. *How to Help Your Child Say "No" to Sexual Pressure*. Waco: Word Books, 1987.

Mc Ginnis, Alan Loy. *The Friendship Factor*. Minneapolis: Augsburg, 1979.

Narramore, Bruce. *Cutting the Cord*. Wheaton: Tyndale, 1990.

Narramore, Bruce. *Help! I'm a Parent*. Grand Rapids: Zondervan, 1972.

Narramore, Bruce. *Why Children Misbehave*. Grand Rapids: Zondervan, 1980.

Norman, Jane and Myron Harris. *The Private Life of the American Teenager*. New York: Rawson, Wade Publishers, Inc., 1981.

Olson, G. Keith. *Why Teenagers Act the Way They Do*. Loveland: Group, 1987.

Richards, Larry. *Youth Ministry*. Grand Rapids: Zondervan, 1971.

Sproul, R. C. *In Search of Dignity*. Ventura: Gospel Light, 1983.

Stonehouse, Catherine M. *Patterns in Moral Development*. Waco: Word, 1980.

Strommen, Merton P. and A. Irene Strommen. *Five Cries of Parents*. San Francisco: Harper and Row, 1985.

Swets, Paul W. *How to Talk So Your Teenager Will Listen*. Waco: Word Books, 1988.

Swindoll, Charles R. *You and Your Child*. New York: Bantam, 1980.

White, John. *Parents in Pain*. Downers Grove: Intervarsity Press, 1979.

Wilson, Earl D. *Try Being a Teenager*. Portland: Multnomah Press, 1982.

Wright, Norman and Rex Johnson. *Communication: Key to Your Teens*. Eugene: Harvest House, 1978.

Yaconelli, Mike and Jim Burns. *High School Ministry.* Grand Rapids: Zondervan, 1986.

PERIODICALS

Coles, Robert. "Children Know about Moral Hypocrisy." *U.S. News and World Report,* 17 February 1986, 61.

Cowley, Geoffrey. "Made to Order Babies." *Newsweek* Special Issue, Winter/Spring 1990, 98.

Dirks, Dennis H. "Moral Maturity and Christian Parenting." *Christian Education Journal* 83 (Winter 1989): 85.

Edmondson, Brad. "Bringing in the Sheaves." *American Demographics,* August 1988.

Gibbs, Nancy. "How America Has Run Out of Time." *Time,* 24 April 1989, 58-60.

Howard, John A. "To Quote." *Youthworker Update,* September 1989, 8.

Lawrence, Rick. "Techno-Teens." *Group,* January 1990, 21.

Marek, Elizabeth. "The Lives of Teenage Mothers." *Harper's,* April 1989, 56.

Menconi, Al with Dave Hart. "Talkin' 'Bout the Way I Feel . . . ." *Christian Parenting Today,* April 1990, 25-27.

Menconi, Al. "News Bits." *Media Update,* November/December 1989, 14.

Menconi, Al. "News Bits." *Media Update,* March/April 1990.

Miller, Dennis. "Christian Teenagers: They're Leaving the Flock." *Moody Monthly*, September 1982, 11-13.

Nigro, Samuel. *U.S. News and World Report*, 21 November 1988, 8.

Petersen, Jim. "The Eclipse of the Gospel." *Discipleship Journal*, January 1990, 12.

Powell, Stewart. "What Entertainers Are Doing to Your Kids." *U.S. News and World Report*, 28 October 1985, 46.

Roehlkepartain, Jolene L. "15 Going on 35." *Group*, April/May 1990, 14-15.

Schimmels, Cliff. "Questions Parents Ask about Schools." *Focus on the Family*, March 1990, 21.

Schultz, Thom. "Missing the Obvious." *Group*, March 1990, 7.

Sussman, Vic. "News You Can Use." *U.S. News and World Report*, 11 September 1989, 70-72.